IMAGES OF ENGLAND

HORSHAM

Horsham Town 1813.

1. Church.
2. Priest's House.
3. Almshouses.
4. Collyer's School.
5. Morth's Gardens.
6. Causeway House.
7. Town Hall (former Market House)
8. Pump Alley.
9. Middle Street.
10. Bishops Burgage House.

Scale of one eighth of a mile.

100 yds.

Drawn from photographic prints of the Inclosure Map.
Alan Siney, Horsham Museum Society. 2005.

IMAGES OF ENGLAND

HORSHAM

SUSAN C. DJABRI

TEMPUS

Frontispiece: Map of Horsham, redrawn from the 1812-1813
Enclosure Map by Alan Siney. This is the earliest detailed map of
the town centre and shows the Carfax with five main roads leading
into it: London Road (the turnpike road from London via Dorking),
North Street (the road to Crawley), South Street (now known as
the Causeway) leading to the parish church, West Street and East
Street (joined by Middle Street). From West Street, the road led to
Guildford and Oxford; while East Street was extended past the Gaol
and became the road to Henfield and Brighton. The key shows
some of the buildings and places of historic interest.

First published 2006

Tempus Publishing Limited
The Mill, Brimscombe Port,
Stroud, Gloucestershire, GL5 2QG
www.tempus-publishing.com

British Library Cataloguing in Publication Data.
A catalogue record for this book is available from the British Library.

ISBN 0 7524 3831 X

Typesetting and origination by Tempus Publishing Limited.
Printed in Great Britain.

Contents

Acknowledgements

Most of the pictures in this book have been drawn from the fine collection of drawings, paintings and photographs, which are jointly owned by Horsham Museum Society and Horsham District Council (Horsham Museum), who have kindly allowed them to be used in this publication. I would especially like to acknowledge the help and support that I have received from Jeremy Knight, the Curator of Horsham Museum, Gavin Stewart, Assistant Curator, and Mike McCole, in assembling and processing the images needed for this book. I would also like to thank Horsham District Council for providing the photograph of Martin Pearson and that of the sundial at dawn, taken by Freda Fowler. Thanks are also due to Horsham Museum Society for permission to use the photographs collected by them. Roger Baker ARPS, chairman of the Horsham Photographic Society, kindly gave permission for the use of those photographs taken by members of the Photographic Society. I am most grateful to Alan Siney for redrawing the map of the town centre from the 1813 Enclosure Map, and allowing me to use it as the frontispiece of this book.

I have also been most fortunate in being able to include some pictures from private sources, by the kind permission of their owners. I would like to thank Prof. A.R. Gardner-Medwin and Dr. David Gardner-Medwin for allowing me to publish photographs of the miniatures of Thomas Charles Medwin and his son Thomas, the Revd Antony Hurst for the silhouettes of Sarah Hurst and Henry Smith, and Brian Slyfield for the engraving of Sir Henry Fletcher from his copy of Manning and Bray's *History of Surrey*. I am indebted to Stan and Chris Sheppard in Zimbabwe for providing a scan of the photograph of Robert Sheppard, Lady Morse for that of Dorothea Hurst, and Neil Chapman for that of the opening of the swimming pool. Doug Murphy from Canada and Mr and Mrs R. Murrell have generously donated pictures of the staff of the Horsham Institution (formerly the workhouse and its hospital) to Horsham Museum, and Norman Hewell, Robert Hull, and Maureen Radbourne have kindly allowed me to scan their precious family photographs. Robert Hull and Patricia Greenwood have given me access to their research into the Hull and Honywood families – a file on the Honywoods is now in the Horsham Museum library. In writing the text, I have drawn on various articles published in recent issues of *Horsham Heritage,* personal information, and a large number of documentary and printed sources.

Introduction

Every picture from the past is a window to a lost world – though some are far more stunning in their effect than others. Once seen, a picture can remain in the mind and shape one's thinking. Without pictures, it is difficult to fully understand the history of a town like Horsham. How can one appreciate the importance of the great lost mansion of Hill's Place, and its park, without the evidence of drawings and maps? Some important modern landmarks have proved to be quite evanescent – the original inner courtyard of Swan Walk and the skyscraper which first housed the Sun Alliance headquarters only lasted for a few years and might be forgotten, unless seen again in photographs. Change and renewal have been a recurrent feature in Horsham's history, even before the recent extensive redevelopment of the whole of Horsham town centre.

The aim of this book is to provide an outline pictorial history of Horsham, at least during the last two centuries, using the Horsham Museum collections as a main resource. We are fortunate to have drawings and paintings to illustrate the period before the invention of photography. The first chapter is concerned with places or institutions that are like a thread running through the town's history – the manor, the parish church, the school, the market, the Borough and the families who controlled the life of the town in earlier centuries. Later chapters are more concerned with the 'movers and shakers' within the town, and people at work or at play. Some photographs illustrate the great social changes brought about by the coming of the railway and the invention of the bicycle or the motor car. Others show the development of important industries such as brick making, or of public institutions like the workhouse and its hospital. Many of the pictures have not previously been published, and are little known.

A conscious decision was taken to concentrate on pictures of people, rather than those of streets and buildings, which have featured in many other books. But in many cases, people and places are inextricably linked: Canon Hodgson will always be remembered as the restorer of St Mary's church in 1864-5. The rebuilding of much of the town centre around 1900, and the people who were active then, are of particular interest, since many people still consider this period, just before the First World War, as the 'golden age' of the town's history. It is also a period particularly well represented in Horsham Museum's photographic archive, as early members of Horsham Museum Society made significant contributions. With so much material to choose from, I had to make difficult decisions on what to include and what to leave out. In the end, I chose those pictures that I felt gave the most authentic impression of life as it was actually lived in Horsham at the time in question. Thus I have generally preferred more informal shots to group photographs, though I have included some of those too. The photographs of Horsham's great and good at the dedication of the Jubilee Fountain in 1897, the Caledonian Society at Beedingwood, and what appears to be the entire indoor and outdoor staff of Coolhurst, are certainly among some of the most striking in the museum's collection.

I have also concentrated on finding early photographs of historic interest, such as the ones of St Mary's church before restoration, and the likenesses of people who are known to have made a mark on the life of the town in their day. These range from the Lord Paramount of the Borough, the 11th Duke of Norfolk, who was responsible for the enclosure of the Common in the early nineteenth century, to the shoemaker, singer and bell-ringer Henry Burstow, whose reminiscences tell us so much about the life of the ordinary working man in Horsham in the nineteenth century. Percy Bysshe Shelley, the great poet and radical, Alfred Shrubb, the champion runner, Thomas Honywood, artist, photographer, archaeologist and captain of the fire brigade, Jarvis Kenrick, the philanthropic curate, and Charlie Price, the drunken pie seller, all have their place in this gallery of Horsham faces.

It has not always been easy to find pictures of people who have been significant. Horsham Museum had a photograph that purported to be of Dorothea Hurst – the author of the first general history of Horsham in 1868 – but this proved to be a false attribution. An authentic portrait kindly supplied by her family showed a quite different person. It is also due to private generosity and modern technology that we have been able to obtain access to some other interesting photographs, like those of the young William Hull, with his peg-leg, and Robert Sheppard, the engineer.

There are fewer photographs from the last fifty years than for the preceding period, for two good reasons. Firstly, there are fewer photographs of good quality in the Museum archive for this period, although the Museum does have two superb collections: the matching series of photographs of the town taken in 1951 and 2000 by Horsham Photographic Society, and another series taken in the 1990s by Ray Luff. However, these were virtually excluded, because Tempus has already published a book using most of the photographs in the Horsham Photographic Society collection, and few of the Luff photographs were suitable for this particular book.

Some of the pictures in this book have a great deal to tell us, on many different levels. The photograph of Henry Padwick probably tells us more about his character and personality than any other document in the Museum archives. The affectionate portrait of Mrs Mann in all her finery, painted by her son, is a rare domestic interior that takes us right inside the Mann household. Although we should not believe that the camera never lies, we can be grateful for the wealth of information that is revealed about life in Horsham in this rich collection of images.

Susan C. Djabri
Horsham, 2006

one

Historic
Places

This painting shows the remnants of the great manor house of Chesworth, built during the Tudor period. The young Catherine Howard lived here with her step-grandmother, the Dowager Duchess of Norfolk, before her marriage to King Henry VIII in 1540, and brief reign as Queen, until her trial and execution in 1542. Much of this house was pulled down in the early seventeenth century, and the part that remained was used as a farmhouse in the eighteenth and nineteeth centuries. Chesworth is a Saxon name, and this suggests that there was a house here before the Norman conquest of 1066. It was probably the most important building in a small settlement known for breeding horses, called Horsham, which was first mentioned in a charter dated 947.

St Mary the Virgin, the parish church of Horsham, lies a little way along the river from Chesworth, and contains remnants of an early Norman church. The present church was built in about 1247, after the parish had been given to the nuns of Rusper Priory as part of their endowment, by the then Lord of the Manor, John de Braose. This early photograph, one of a number taken by Henry Padwick, junior, dates from before the 1864-5 restoration and shows the south aisle and Shelley Chapel in their original form.

Right: Another of Henry Padwick's photographs shows the tomb of Thomas de Braose, who lived at Chesworth and died in 1395. He was the last of the male descendants of William de Braose, who was given the lordship of Horsham and the surrounding area by King William I, the Norman conqueror. The photograph also shows a large monument placed over the tomb, which disappeared at the time of the 1864-5 restoration. This was possibly the 'magnificent' memorial to Lt-Gen. Henry Smith, which was said to be in St Mary's church in 1800 (see p.23).

Below: Elizabeth Delves, who died in childbirth in 1654, was commemorated as a model daughter, wife and mother by this beautiful tomb, carved by Edward Marshall, Master of the Mason's Company. She was the only child of Hall Ravenscroft, MP for Horsham, who was a supporter of Parliament against the King, during the Civil War.

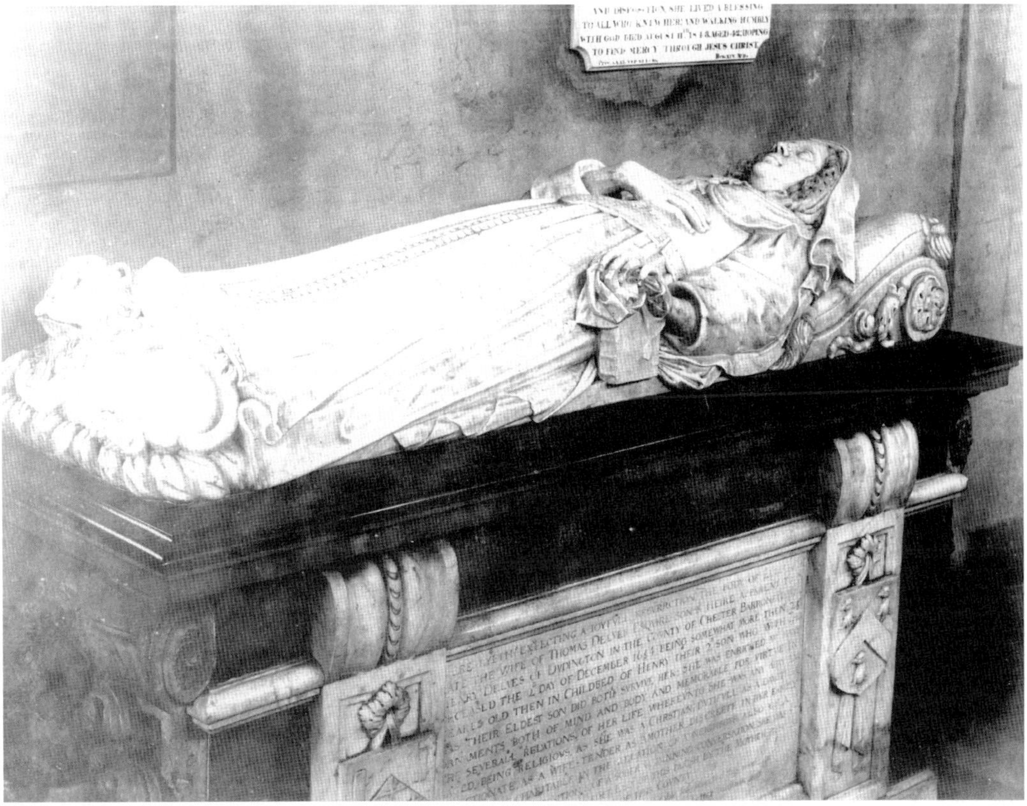

Henry Padwick's photograph of the nave, before restoration in 1864-5, gives us an extraordinary glimpse of St Mary's church as it was then, with its large box pews and heavy galleries, which eventually caused the whole building to lean to the north at a dangerous angle. Ownership of a pew bestowed considerable social status in the eighteenth and early nineteenth centuries, and pew places were bought and sold as family fortunes fluctuated. Sarah Hurst, whose diary of the years 1759 to 1762 gives a vivid glimpse of life in Horsham at this period, greatly admired the sermons of the Vicar, the Revd Thomas Hutchinson, which were preached from the large central pulpit. He was an eminent classical scholar, whose translations of Aeschylus were much admired in their day.

This is a rare photograph of the Priest's House, an important medieval building which stood at the east end of St Mary's church, and figures in many drawings and paintings. The parish priest lived there before the building of a vicarage, first mentioned in 1724. The Priest's House was restored during the nineteenth century, and not demolished until about 1895.

The original building of Collyer's School, here shown in a woodcut by Howard Dudley, was Horsham's earliest educational establishment. Founded as a grammar school for poor boys in his native town by a rich London mercer called Richard Collyer, who died in 1532, it was an active and successful school in the sixteenth and seventeenth centuries. The school was in a state of decline during most of the eighteenth century, and by 1807 it had no pupils. It was reorganised as a 'Free School' in 1813, to provide an elementary education for sixty poor boys. Dudley's woodcut appeared in *The History and Antiquities of Horsham*, published in 1836. This was the first book devoted to the history of the town and was written and illustrated entirely by himself at the age of sixteen.

An early photograph of the Carfax, looking south. It shows the large open area where the cattle market and town fairs were held from the thirteenth to the nineteenth centuries. Remnants of the grass from the part known as Gaol Green can be seen in the foreground. Horsham was the seat of the Sussex County Gaol for three centuries, from about 1531 to 1835. During that time there were at least three gaol buildings; the first in North Street, and the second, built in 1640, on the north side of the Carfax, with the Gaol Green in front of it. John Howard, the prison reformer, condemned this gaol as filthy and unsafe when he visited it in 1774, and a new 'model' gaol was then built in East Street.

Pump Alley, just off Market Square, was at the hub of seventeenth-century Horsham. It housed two important inns, the Talbot and Wonder, which had large stables. At this time Horsham was an important staging post, where travellers between London and the coast could rest and change horses. There is a blurred figure of a woman energetically scrubbing the front doorstep of her cottage, which recalls William Cobbett's comment in 1823, in one of his rural rides, that Horsham was a 'very clean' and 'nice, solid' country town.

This reworked sketch of the Market House, by Thomas Mann or his son George, from an earlier drawing, shows it as it was before 1812, when it was rebuilt as the Town Hall. The Market House was used by farmers' wives to sell their butter, cheese and poultry on market days. The lower part was boarded up to serve as a courtroom for the Assizes or Quarter Sessions, or as a theatre when strolling players came to the town. The judges complained that the Market House was draughty and uncomfortable, and it was rebuilt so that the Assizes, and the profitable business they brought to the town, would remain in Horsham.

The Borough of Horsham came into existence in the early thirteenth century, and first sent two members to Parliament in 1295. Causeway House is one of the old burgage houses, whose owners had the right to vote (a system that later became corrupt). Now the home of Horsham Museum, this house has been occupied by many notable Horsham people through the centuries. Among the most prominent were the barrister, landowner and long-serving MP for Horsham, Robert Hurst, and his sister Sarah, the diarist. This painting by an unknown artist is one of the earliest known images of the building, dating from the mid-nineteenth century.

Bishops, one of the finest medieval burgage houses in Horsham, stands on the south-east corner of East Street and Denne Road, where it is thought that there was a Saxon settlement. The artist, Maria Hurst, was one of the daughters of Robert Henry Hurst, senior, who was elected MP for Horsham in 1832.

North Chapel, in North Street, was owned in 1545 by the religious fraternity of St John and St Anne, founded in 1457, under the patronage of Thomas Hoo of Roffey. The building was extended in the seventeenth century, and divided into three cottages. It was later owned by Miss Elizabeth Gatford, a 'lady of fortune and pity', who died in 1799, leaving many charitable donations.

Denne House, a Jacobean mansion on Denne Hill, about a mile south of the town, was built
in 1606 by Sir Thomas Eversfield, who had prospered as an ironmaster at Worth. His daughter
Bridget married into the Shelley family, who owned land in the Horsham area. Another daughter
called Timothy (then a girl's name) married William Browne, the poet of the Inner Temple, whose
work influenced Milton and Keats.

Charles Eversfield succeeded to the Denne estates after the death of his great-uncle Anthony
Eversfield, MP for Horsham from 1679 to 1690. This portrait of Charles with his first wife, Mary
Duncombe, was probably painted at the time of their marriage in 1702, in St Paul's Cathedral,
by Sir Godfrey Kneller or one of his circle. Charles was MP for Horsham (or Sussex) from 1705
until 1738. As a local magistrate, he proved rather negligent in his pursuit of smugglers. But he was
hailed as a generous benefactor by prisoners in Horsham Gaol, since he sent them a large joint of
beef every week!

Hill's Place was built around 1630 on the western outskirts of the town by John Middleton, a powerful Sussex ironmaster with business interests in the Midlands. His son Thomas was an MP for Horsham during the Civil War, but was suspected of Royalist sympathies after a brief uprising in Horsham in 1648 and heavily fined. Hill's Place was bought in 1668 by John Machell, whose daughter Isabella married Arthur Ingram, later 3rd Viscount Irwin, of Temple Newsam in Yorkshire. John Machell left Hill's Place to his grandson Rich Ingram, who became 5th Viscount Irwin. His younger brother Henry, 7th Viscount Irwin, gained complete political control of the Borough of Horsham in 1737.

This map by Lancelot 'Capability' Browne shows his suggestions for improvements to the park at Hill's Place, centring around a large lake, formed by damming the river Arun, and a cascade. These plans were carried out in the 1770s, after Charles Ingram, 9th Viscount Irwin, had married an heiress with a fortune of £60,000. After her husband's early death in 1778, Lady Irwin held a life interest in the Horsham estates, and the town became known as her 'pocket borough'.

'The Remains of Hill's Place'. This painting by an unknown artist dates from about 1830, and shows Hill's Place as it was then. After Lady Irwin's death in 1807, the 11th Duke of Norfolk bought Hill's Place and thirty-eight Horsham burgage properties from her heirs, in 1811. In 1820, the 12th Duke pulled down the mansion, leaving only the earlier Elizabethan farmhouse and its Georgian extension, and sold off the land in sixteen lots. The great lake was drained and the park returned to farmland.

This photograph of Hill's Place shows the Elizabethan farmhouse, which was eventually demolished in the 1920s. The Georgian extension behind it survived as a private house until the 1980s, when the site was redeveloped.

This watercolour, entitled 'A Bridge near Horsham', was painted by George Robertson around 1765, and was recently purchased by Horsham Museum, with generous assistance from the National Art Collections Fund. It is thought to show the turnpike road from London crossing the Red River near Warnham Mill, about two miles from the town centre. In the background are the Warnham floodgates, which were part of the system that enabled the flow of water to the millwheel to be controlled by the miller. The building of the turnpike roads was of great significance to Horsham, as the improved roads made the town an important coaching centre at the beginning of the nineteenth century.

A photograph of the Warnham floodgates taken in the 1890s makes an interesting comparison with the painting above. In 1906, the floodgates were breached, and hundreds of fish were left stranded – an event recorded by contemporary postcards. A century earlier, the millpond was part of the Shelley estates and the young Percy Bysshe Shelley made it his playground, learning to sail and fish in its waters. His earliest known letter is about a picnic he wanted to share with his cousin, Thomas Medwin, during a day at Warnham pond.

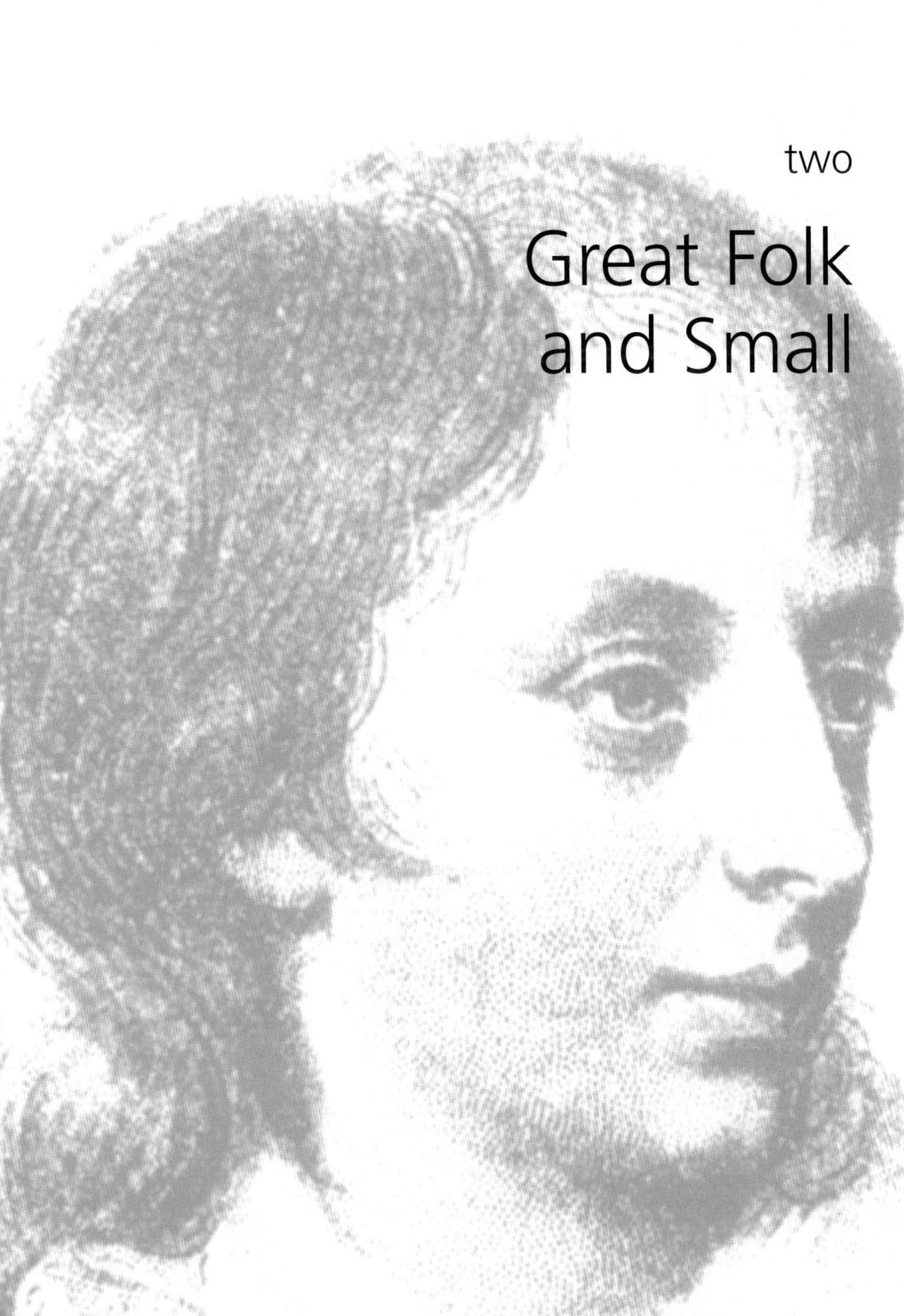

two

Great Folk
and Small

Charles, 11th Duke of Norfolk, was Lord Paramount of the Borough of Horsham from 1785 until his death in 1815. In the 1790 parliamentary election, his political agents, Robert Hurst and Thomas Charles Medwin, spent £70,000 and used devious tactics to win the election for the Duke's candidates, but the result was overturned. The Duke was not able to gain full political control of Horsham until he bought the Irwin estates in 1811, for £91,475. He promoted an act for the enclosure of Horsham and Roffey Commons in 1812, but only recovered about £10,000 from the sale of land allotted to him. The enclosure is now considered to have been of long-term benefit to the town.

Sir Henry Fletcher, a former director of the East India Company and MP for Cumberland, was an important burgage holder in Horsham (in the right of his wife), who supported the Duke of Norfolk in the 1790 election campaign. In 1768, he married Catherine Lintot, sole heiress to family estates in Horsham and Southwater and the publishing business founded by her grandfather Bernard, in London. Sir Henry took a considerable interest in the Horsham estates, while Lady Fletcher established a Christmas charity for poor people in Southwater. Their descendants still own land there.

Robert Hurst, the Horsham lawyer, served the Duke of Norfolk as steward of his manors in Norfolk and Suffolk, and was the Duke's legal adviser and trustee of the Shelley estates before becoming MP for Steyning and then Horsham. He became the largest landowner in the town after buying up the majority of the land made available by the enclosure of Horsham and Roffey Commons in 1812-1813. But how was he able to afford the £10,000 necessary to make these enormous purchases?

Above left: Robert Hurst's elder sister Sarah kept a fascinating diary about her life in Horsham between 1759 and 1762. In April 1762, she married Henry Smith, then a captain in the Marines, in Slinfold, but the marriage remained a secret until the end of the year, when she prepared to join Henry, now promoted to Major, in Plymouth. She returned to Horsham as a childless widow in 1798 and died in 1808, leaving some £10,000, which she had amassed through care and frugality, to her brother Robert.

Above right: Sarah's husband, Lt-Gen. Henry Smith, was one of Horsham's most eminent soldiers, and was said to have had a 'magnificent' memorial in St Mary's church in 1800, although only an inscription on the north wall of the tower now records his life and character. He fought in the Seven Years' War and served as Colonel Commandant of the Royal Marines at Portsmouth from 1772 to 1791. His niece, Maria, who was Robert Hurst's wife, and her children, were the main beneficiaries of his will, after Sarah's death.

Timothy Shelley was elected MP for Horsham in 1790 as one of the Duke of Norfolk's candidates, but was unseated in 1792, on appeal. He became MP for New Shoreham in 1802, and held the seat until 1817. He was the largest landowner in the Horsham area, inheriting the Stammerham estates of his mother and those of his father, Sir Bysshe Shelley, throughout West Sussex. He invested in turnpikes and agricultural improvements, and generally maintained good relations with his tenants.

Percy Bysshe Shelley, son of Timothy, was born in 1792 and is shown here as a child growing up at Field Place in Warnham. As the expected heir to his father's and grandfather's estates, his rift with his family in 1812 caused them bitter disappointment, and his early death in 1822 was a tragedy that cast a very long shadow. His reputation as a great poet and radical writer was only established many years after his death, and he was long disregarded by Horsham townspeople, who clung to their prejudices concerning his ideas and way of life.

This sketch of Shelley's study, by the artist Thomas Mann, was found in the catalogue of a sale of furniture at Field Place in 1848. It was probably here that Shelley wrote his earliest poems, some with his sister Elizabeth. They were published under the title of *Victor and Cazire* while he was still a schoolboy, but the book was withdrawn from sale when it was found to mistakenly contain a copy of a published poem by another writer. Shelley was expelled from Oxford in 1811 when he and Thomas Jefferson Hogg published a short pamphlet entitled *The Necessity of Atheism*.

A miniature of Lt John Pilfold, who commanded HMS *Ajax* at the Battle of Trafalgar in 1805, and was subsequently made a Companion of the Order of the Bath. He came from a well-established Horsham family and was the brother of Timothy Shelley's wife, Elizabeth. He proved to be a kind uncle to Percy Bysshe after his elopement with his first wife, Harriet Westbrook, in 1812. He supplied the young couple with money after Timothy Shelley had cut off his son's allowance, and tried unsuccessfully to bring the family together again.

Thomas Charles Medwin was a very active and enterprising lawyer and political agent who was the Duke of Norfolk's steward, Town Clerk of Horsham, and land agent to Sir Henry Fletcher. For twenty-five years he was the pivot of nearly everything that went on in Horsham, until he lost his position with the Duke and quarelled with Timothy Shelley, his wife's cousin, in 1812. Though he served as an active school warden of Collyer's School and continued his legal practice in partnership with his youngest son Pilfold, he was heavily in debt when he died in 1829.

The Revd George Marshall was curate of Horsham for over thirty years, and chaplain of Horsham Gaol. He was a friend of Thomas Charles Medwin and Timothy Shelley. Though somewhat eccentric in his manner and ideas, he founded the National School in the church porch in 1812, which proved of benefit to the town, at a time when Collyer's School was in serious decline. (This painting is on loan to Horsham Museum from West Sussex County Council).

"Though Prisoners here we be,
Yet shall our minds be free
chearly to sing
Soon may we Rence depart
And may base Bonaparte
Take our place—under Smart
God save the King"

Smart the name of the Keeper

I am much obliged to you
Gentlemen, for your kind offer
but I would just as soon have
any thing to do with the Devil himself!

Loyal Prisoners at Horsham
Commemorating his Majestys Birth Day,

The new 'model' gaol in East Street contained two separate sections: one for debtors, who were confined until they could pay their creditors, and the other for prisoners awaiting trial for criminal offences. This jolly drawing shows some of the debtor prisoners celebrating the birthday of King George III in 1804. The accompanying verses express their wish that 'base Bonaparte' should take their place under their gaoler, Samuel Smart. The artist was G.M. Woodward, who led 'an irregular life', and apparently died destitute in 1809. Perhaps he was a debtor inmate of Horsham Gaol in 1804, as he appears to have inside knowledge of what went on there!

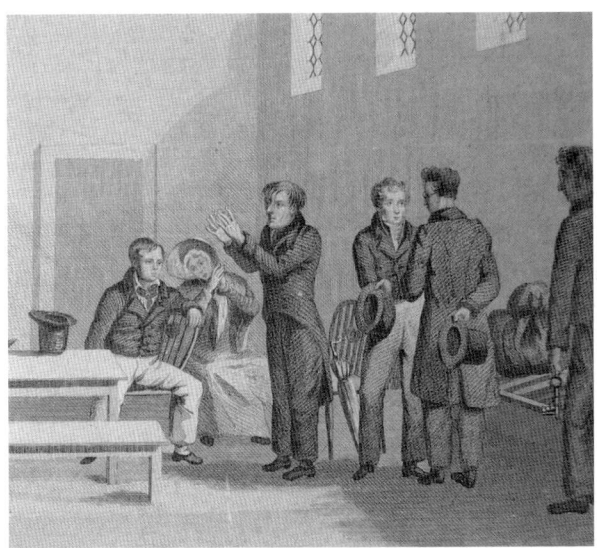

William Holloway is seen here in the prison infirmary with a visiting minister and other officials, during the grim final hours before his execution. He was sentenced to death in 1831 for the murder of his wife. His mother is seated beside him, and the gaoler, Mr Doswell, is on the far right. Between 1822 and 1845, public executions of convicted criminals from Sussex took place on gallows set up outside Horsham Gaol in East Street. Hawkers took advantage of the assembled crowd to ply their trade at these 'Hanging Fairs'.

Above left: This miniature is one of the earliest known portraits of a Horsham woman from a tradesman's family. The pinchbeck brooch and mourning ring commemorate the death of Prudence Sheppard in 1811, aged sixty. She was the wife of Stringer Sheppard, a butcher who lived in Market Square, and the mother of eight children. Her father, John Smart, was a millwright, timber-merchant and landlord of the Dog and Bacon Inn on Horsham Common in the early 1770s.

Above right: This little token commemorates the Horsham Peace Dinner on 11 August 1814, a great public celebration to mark the capture of Napoleon Bonaparte and his exile to Elba – held before he escaped and returned to fight the battle of Waterloo! William Sheppard, the eldest son of Stringer and Prudence, was on the organising committee for the dinner, recruiting men to carve and serve the large joints of beef provided on long tables in George Waller's field.

The Town Mill, the oldest corn mill in the town, was in the hands of the Smart and Sheppard families for over a century. In 1751, John Smart bought a half share in the mill with John Michell, a plumber, who laid some waterpipes from the river Arun to the Causeway. His son-in-law, Stringer Sheppard, became sole lessee in 1803, and Stringer's son William worked there as miller for over thirty years. William Sheppard was one of the last Bailiffs of the Borough of Horsham in 1835.

three

Hard
Times

In this drawing by an unknown artist, probably dating from the 1830s, St Mary's church and the Priest's House, with the old parish workhouse on the far left of the picture, are shown in a state of considerable dilapidation. Plants are sprouting from the roofs, and there is a large crack in the east wall of the church. This was a time of great poverty and hardship in Horsham, as elsewhere, with little effective local leadership. There were serious agricultural disturbances throughout southern England in the winter of 1830, which led to the fall of the Duke of Wellington's government and provoked widespread fears of a violent revolution.

This early photograph, taken by Henry Padwick, junior, shows the chancel of St Mary's church before the restoration of 1864-5. This was the scene of a riot over the payment of tithes, between an angry mob of labourers and the Vicar and Robert Hurst, the main titheholders, on 18 November 1830. The altar rail was 'o'erleaped' and there were fears of bloodshed before the Vicar and Mr Hurst agreed to make some concessions on the payment of tithes (which were never put into effect). Troops were called in to restore order, after the townspeople showed sympathy with the rioters and refused to sign up as special constables.

This painting by Fred Burstow, called 'The Piemen', shows Charles Price and John Hamilton (or Oberton) Smith, who sold pies and buns in the Carfax in the 1830s. John Smith was a pastry-cook who lived in the Bishopric. Henry Burstow said, in his *Reminiscences of Horsham,* that Charlie 'Patch' Price was the last man to be put in stocks in 1834 for drunkenness, but had frequently been put there before for the same offence. He described him as 'an ugly little brass-whisker'd man with a club foot; dressed in a pot hat, red handkerchief, white smock frock, drab breeches, and white stockings; on his good foot he wore a low shoe with a flash buckle; on his other foot he had a thick boot'.

This caricature of an early Horsham policeman, Police Constable Porter, was probably also drawn by Fred Burstow. Before the establishment of a professional police force in 1839, Horsham had to rely solely on part-time parish constables to maintain law and order, with the help of the stocks and the whipping post. While the constables might arrest criminals within their parish, they were unable to bring them to court unless the victim of the crime was prepared to pay for the prosecution. A Society for Prosecuting Thieves was set up in Horsham in 1785, which provided a fund to subsidise the prosecution of such cases.

The Revd Jarvis Kenrick, curate of Horsham, is seen here in a very early photograph. In 1840, he paid for a new building for the boys' National School in North Street, next door to the new St Mark's Chapel, out of his own resources. He also gave £500 and raised matching funds to buy the old parish workhouse in 1842, which was then converted into almshouses. He preached a powerful sermon on Good Friday 1844, deploring public attendance at John Lawrence's execution, due to be held on the following day. As a result, many people stayed away and schoolchildren were taken up to Denne Park during the event.

George Bax Holmes, an early collector of dinosaur fossils, was a Quaker whose father and grandfather were cutlers with a business in the Carfax. In 1840, George identified some fossilised dinosaur bones, found in the sandstone dug out during the building of St Mark's Chapel in North Street, and named them the 'Great Horsham Iguanodon'. He also found the remains of a plesiosaurus in St Leonard's Forest. His important collection of 767 fossils, which has now achieved worldwide renown, was sold to Brighton Corporation in 1887 by his daughter for a mere £55!

An early photograph of W.D. Baker's watch and clock shop in Middle Street (next door to Glaysher's the ironmonger). Mr Baker moved to West Street in 1858, so this picture must have been taken before that date. Perhaps it is he who is standing on the doorstep of his shop, greeting one of his customers.

This is a rare photograph of the interior of St Mark's Chapel as it was originally built, with the 'judicious ornamentation' that was added to the bare whitewashed walls in the 1860s. The Revd A.H. Bridges, who served as the first minister there from 1841 to 1858, paid for considerable extensions in 1871, when the spire was also built in memory of his daughter. St Mark's was closed in 1936 to help provide for a new church in the east part of the town. The old church was pulled down in 1989-1990 as part of the town centre redevelopment, but the spire was retained after a vigorous protest campaign. A new St Mark's church has been built in North Horsham to serve the greatly extended community there.

Left and below: William Pirie was appointed as headmaster of Collyer's School in 1822, as a very young man, and remained in office until his death in 1868. During this period, he managed to get the old Tudor school replaced by a modern building and restored the school's reputation. William built a terrace of fourteen houses off the Carfax, to provide for his retirement, and was a familiar sight driving around Horsham in his donkey cart. He is now commemorated by Lorne McKean's statue in Pirie's Place, the modern shopping centre that has replaced the old terrace and central market.

Opposite: Henry Padwick, senior – lawyer, moneylender, political agent, and speculator – was one of the most able and active men in Horsham in the mid-nineteenth century, but was both feared and disliked. He managed the Hurst estates after Robert Henry Hurst, senior was declared bankrupt in 1845, and acted as political agent for W.R. Seymour Fitzgerald, an Irishman who bought the Holbrook estate in order to be able to stand in the 1847 election. Henry Padwick lent money to the young Edward Tredcroft, and then foreclosed on the debt, forcing the sale of the Manor House in the Causeway and all other Tredcroft estates in Sussex, many of which he acquired for himself in 1856. He set up a racing stable at Findon, and gambled heavily at the races. A note on the back of this photograph suggests that he might have committed suicide in 1879.

This lively drawing by Fred Burstow depicts the 1847 parliamentary election, the most corrupt in Horsham's history, which brought the town national disgrace. The opposing candidates were the Tory, Seymour Fitzgerald, and Sir John Jervis, Attorney General, who held Liberal views. Both candidates plied the voters with drink in unlimited quantities to win their support. Sir John won the poll, but the result

was contested and he was unseated for 'treating' the voters. Fitzgerald won the subsequent by-election but he too was unseated for the same reason. In 1852, Fitzgerald eventually managed to win the seat, and served as Under Secretary for Foreign Affairs from 1858 to 1859 in Lord Derby's government.

Pilfold Medwin was the youngest son of Thomas Charles Medwin and worked all his life in Horsham as a lawyer, land agent, and election agent for Liberal candidates. He was a kindly man who spent many years struggling to pay off the debts incurred by his father and elder brother, yet he was always ready to help those in need. He served as a 'Guardian of the Poor' and sat on many other committees. Pilfold was nicknamed 'The Man of Horsham' by one of the many townspeople who had cause to be grateful to him. When he died in 1880, he was the last surviving burgess of the old Borough constituency.

This poster is for the sale of Pilfold Medwin's furniture and library of 600 books in 1848. Henry Padwick, formerly a close friend, sent in the bailiffs to recover a debt which Pilfold had not been able to repay. This cost Pilfold his old home and office, on the corner of West Street and the Carfax, and he spent the rest of his life in lodgings in London Road. Medwin Walk, off the Carfax, is a former part of London Road now named after the Medwin family.

This tiny pocket book was a pirated edition of the first substantial English collection of Percy Bysshe Shelley's poems, published in 1839. Until then, most Horsham people would not have had an opportunity to read much of his work. During his lifetime, Sir Timothy Shelley tried to suppress any use or promotion of his son's name, but this publication persuaded him to allow his son's widow, Mary Wollstonecraft Shelley, to publish an annotated collection of his poems in 1840. After Sir Timothy's death in 1844, Mary lived for a while at Field Place and published an authoritative three-volume edition of Shelley's poems in 1847.

Thomas Medwin, Pilfold's elder brother, published the first full-length biography of Percy Bysshe Shelley, also in 1847. This contained his own first-hand memories of the poet's childhood and early youth in Horsham, and the artistic circle in which Shelley lived in Pisa in 1821. Thomas sought financial support for this venture from Henry Padwick, but faced opposition from Mary Shelley, who feared that he might damage the more favourable image of Shelley that she was trying to promote. In 1865, Thomas returned to Horsham to escape his creditors and live with his brother Pilfold, who cared for him until he died in 1869.

Henry Michell was one of Horsham's most successful businessmen and entrepreneurs in the Victorian period. He started his working life in Horsham as a brewer, but also became a brick-maker and property developer. He bought Horsham Gaol in East Street, after it had been closed in 1845, and opened it to public view before he pulled it down. He carefully recycled all the materials to be sold or used elsewhere, rebuilding the West Street brewery and laying out Park Square on the site of the gaol, although this imaginative building scheme was later ruined by the extension of the railway right through the middle! Henry took an active part in local affairs: in 1851, he organised a railway trip to London for 380 Horsham schoolchildren to see the Great Exhibition.

This early photograph of the northern side of the Carfax, taken by Thomas Honywood in 1855, is of considerable historic interest. The gabled house to the right of the pedimented Fountain and Cock brewery is the Richmond Hotel, which stood on the site of the second Horsham Gaol, built in 1640. After the new 'model' gaol was completed in 1779, the old gaol was sold to a schoolmaster, Richard Thornton, who had a private academy there from about 1774 to 1814. By 1840 it appears to have been largely rebuilt as the Richmond Hotel, and it also housed Horsham's Literary Institution. The hotel was bought by Henry Michell, in 1853, and it became his family home after considerable alterations in 1868.

This drawing of Horsham Gaol by Thomas Honywood was commissioned by Henry Michell before he pulled it down, thinking that 'the structure of the Gaol might one day be matter for speculation among natives yet unborn'. Thomas was doubtless taught how to draw by his father John, who was a surveyor. John supervised the building of a new malthouse for Henry Michell's West Street brewery.

This postcard, which is said to show two Horsham postmen, is actually a photograph taken in 1850 by Thomas Honywood of his father John and his brother, John Morth Honywood, who was a builder. Thomas is believed to have introduced photography to Horsham, and it is fortunate that several of his early photographs have survived as a series of postcards, published in Horsham more than fifty years later.

Left: This photograph, also taken by Thomas Honywood in 1850, is one of the first to show ordinary working men from the Horsham area. These woodcutters probably worked on one of the large estates surrounding the town. The proper care of their timber was one of a landowner's main concerns, as it provided a useful and continuing source of income, if carefully managed.

Below: The new age of the railway brought increased opportunity and greater prosperity to Horsham, but it also had its dangers. This lively drawing of a train collision near the iron bridge over East Street, on a snowy day, dates from 1866. The mid-Sussex line was extended to Pulborough and Petworth in 1857, and other lines were built to Guildford in 1860 and Dorking in 1862, making Horsham an important railway junction during the next century.

four

Agents of
Progress

The Birth Place of Thomas Mann.

Above: Thomas Mann, the Horsham artist, was born in this building in North Street in 1834. He was the son and namesake of a druggist who invented a patent medicine, which was still being sold as a popular remedy in the 1890s. As his father was so successful, it seems that the younger Thomas had ample opportunity to develop his artistic talents, although he also trained as a chemist and eventually took over the family business.

Left: This portrait of his mother is one of Thomas Mann's most accomplished works, painted in 1865. It seems very likely that she was sitting in the parlour of the family home, shown above, so the houses in the background are presumably those of North Street. It is a rare domestic interior, at a time when most photographic portraits were made in a studio against a false background.

Above and right: Henry Padwick, junior, was his father's only son, a barrister and local magistrate who was also an enthusiastic amateur photographer. His photographs of St Mary's church, taken in 1862, before its restoration, are a valuable historical record, and he presented the church with its Willis organ in 1865. In the 1860s, he lived at Wimblehurst, a large Victorian mansion, with his elegant wife, Jane Eleanor Tooke, from East Grinstead. Of their seven sons, one became a doctor, another a tea-planter and the third an artist.

Canon John Fisher Hodgson is seen here with his wife and four daughters. The two gentlemen in the back row are his younger brother, the Revd Henry William Hodgson, Rector of Ashwell, Herts, and his son-in-law, the Revd Edmund Willis, then priest in charge of St Mark's Chapel. Canon Hodgson served as vicar of Horsham for forty-three years, from 1840 to 1883, and oversaw the restoration of St Mary's church in 1864-1865, after the fabric was found to be seriously insecure. In his early years he caused some controversy in Horsham, as he was a supporter of the 'High Church' Oxford Movement, which was disliked by some members of his congregation, including William Pirie and Henry Michell.

This photograph of Canon Hodgson playing chess with his brother was probably taken on the same day as the one above, as they appear to be dressed the same in both pictures. It seems likely that both photographs date from about 1880, and were perhaps taken to commemorate the fortieth anniversary of Canon Hodgson's ministry.

This drawing of St Mary's church during the course of restoration gives a striking impression of the extent of the work involved. The roof and old galleries had to be removed so that the pillars and walls of the nave, which were listing dangerously to the north, could be jacked up and restored to the perpendicular. This very difficult engineering feat was successfully achieved under the supervision of the architect, Mr S.S. Teulon, and was watched with great curiosity by many townspeople. The window at the east end was rebuilt in perpendicular style, and the south aisle was extended.

The interior of St Mary's church after restoration shows the wall paintings of the Last Supper and the Ascension, which were repainted when traces of the original medieval wall paintings were found after the removal of the gallery at the back of the church. This photograph makes an interesting comparison with that on p.12.

Robert Henry Hurst, junior, was a distinguished lawyer who was first elected as a Liberal MP for Horsham in 1865, when he defeated Seymour Fitzgerald. Robert inherited all the land bought by his grandfather, but his father's bankruptcy in 1845 made it very difficult for him to manage his estates and repay outstanding debts. He campaigned unsuccessfully for Horsham to adopt public health reforms in the 1860s, but in 1875 he was elected as the first chairman of the Local Board of Health. In his latter years, he became a great benefactor to the town and was known as Horsham's 'Grand Old Man' when he died in 1905.

An early photograph of Park House, without later Victorian additions, which was the main home of the Hurst family from 1799 to 1927. It was built in North Street by John Wicker, who was an MP for Horsham between 1701 and 1713. The house is now the headquarters of Horsham District Council, while its gardens form part of Horsham Park, which contains the public swimming pool, tennis courts and other facilities.

Dorothea Hurst, a younger sister of Robert Henry Hurst, junior, and a highly intelligent woman, researched and wrote the first detailed history of Horsham. In her early life, Dorothea accompanied her father when he was forced to live abroad to escape his creditors, and she also cared for her younger sister Augusta, who died of consumption in 1855. This photograph was perhaps taken then, as she appears to be dressed in deep mourning. In 1869 she got permission to use a small iron building in Roffey Street, north east of the suburb of Roffey, where she ran a school for fifty very poor pupils. Dorothea walked out to Roffey each day from her home in the Causeway to teach the children herself.

Horsham:

ITS

HISTORY AND ANTIQUITIES.

WITH ILLUSTRATIONS.

LONDON : WILLIAM MACINTOSH,
24, PATERNOSTER ROW.
1868.

Title page of the first edition of *Horsham: Its History and Antiquities*, published anonymously in 1868, with only the monogram 'DH' hinting at its authorship. A second edition appeared under Dorothea Hurst's name in 1886, which contained fuller botanical notes and a glossary of Sussex dialect.

This 'Ape' cartoon shows Sir Seymour Fitzgerald – knighted when he became governor of Bombay after his defeat by Robert Henry Hurst in 1865 – when he returned to Horsham and turned the tables on his former opponent at the 1874 election. The 1872 Ballot Act had abolished the corrupt old system of 'open elections', and brought in the secret ballot, which is the foundation of modern democracy. But Sir Seymour did not remain long in his former seat – he had to resign when he was appointed Chief Charity Commissioner and Mr Hurst was re-elected in 1875, at what became known as the 'Teetotal Election'.

The Town Hall covered with posters at the time of the 1876 by-election, called after Robert Henry Hurst was unseated (rather unfairly) because of irregularities committed by his agent. The Liberal, Major James Clifton Brown of Holmbush, was the winner, though there seem to be more posters for his Tory opponent, Sir Hardinge Giffard, the Solicitor General. The huge output of printed matter at this election meant that professional bill-posters from London and Brighton had to be brought in to do the work.

Right: Robert Sheppard, nephew of William Sheppard the miller, was trained as a surveyor and engineer. He worked in London for a time, before returning to Horsham, where he set up a professional practice. He was appointed secretary and superintendent of Horsham Gas Works, and also became engineer-in-chief of Horsham Waterworks, a private company established in 1866 to bring piped water to the town. He was known as 'Churchwarden Sheppard' because he served as churchwarden of St Mark's for many years. He was a prominent Tory activist in the 1875 election, and also served as an agent for insurance companies and building societies.

Below: Richard Cragg, at top left, was acting headmaster of Collyer's School from 1869 to 1883, with the usher, James Williams, and boys from Group 7. Cragg was considered the 'ideal teacher' by one of his pupils, although the subjects he taught were very limited and he used the rod. James Williams succeeded Richard Cragg and was the last headmaster of Collyer's School on its original site in Denne Road.

William Hull, senior, rose from poverty to become a respected Horsham tradesman. He came to Horsham from Slinfold, where his family had been on parish relief, in 1841, at the age of nineteen, and found work in Henry Michell's brewery. His widowed mother was given a place in the Normandy almshouses. In the 1850s, with his wife's help, he also began to sell fruit, vegetables and home-made cakes in Horsham market, before establishing a greengrocer's shop and bakery in West Street. In this photograph, probably taken in the 1880s, William is shown wearing a gentleman's embroidered smoking hat, popularly known as a 'thinking cap'.

Mary Hull, *née* Nicholson, came from a large farming family in Shipley and married William Hull in 1849. During the next eleven years, like many Victorian wives, she bore seven children while helping him to establish their business.

Right: William Hull, junior, the eldest son of William and Mary, was even more energetic and successful than his parents. He lost the lower part of his left leg when he knocked over a loaded shotgun but, despite his peg leg, he managed to teach gymnastics and play cricket! He established a corn merchant's business, and also became landlord of the Crown Inn, where his wife Emma was responsible for the daily management. William was active in many local societies, including the Bonfire Society and the Horsham Amateur Athletic Association. He was elected as a member of Horsham Urban District Council soon after it was set up in 1894.

Below: In this photograph taken at a tradesmen's cricket match in 1889, William Hull, junior, can be seen in the middle row, looking to his right, and wearing a light-coloured waistcoat. It is not really clear whether this group is of spectators or players, or both, though the men in long white coats are probably umpires. It seems to have been a warm day as most of the men are in their shirtsleeves, and wearing a wide variety of headgear!

Henry Burstow, the famous shoemaker, bell-ringer and folk-singer, who could sing 420 songs from memory, is here shown on a postcard by Bon Marché of Queen Street, which includes the verses that William Albery wrote about him. Albery established a fund to keep Burstow from having to go into the workhouse in his old age, by publishing his *Reminiscences of Horsham* in 1911. This book recounts Burstow's personal memories of life in Horsham during the nineteenth century.

I am an old cobbler of eighty-five
And to keep merry I still contrive,
I laugh and sing but I seldom swear,
For I like to see happiness everywhere.
In Horsham Town I was born and bred,
Was schooled, learned ringing, went courting and wed,
Enjoyed my rights, endured my wrongs,
Lived all my life, learned all my songs.
I'm poor in pocket but rich in content,
The fruits of an ill-paid life well spent,
Now slow of limb and dull of eye,
I enjoy life still, though ready to die.
W.A.

Opposite above: In this photograph of West Street, taken in 1880, some modern buildings can be seen, though the old Red Lion building on the right shows its medieval origins. The lady on the right is looking at the windows of George Duke's Emporium, which was in the building where the Medwin family previously had their home and office. On the opposite side of the road, the new building of Hunt Brothers, with its classical pillars, and the bow windows further down the street show where rebuilding has taken place.

Opposite below: The Salvage Corps of Horsham Volunteer Fire Brigade had eleven members led by Mr R. Gilburd as Superintendent, in 1874, and premises next to the original Hurst Arms (or Black Jack) in North Street. The Fire Brigade also had an Engineers Corps and an Escape Corps, all supported by voluntary subscriptions. The men drilled regularly, since fire was an ever-present danger in both town and countryside.

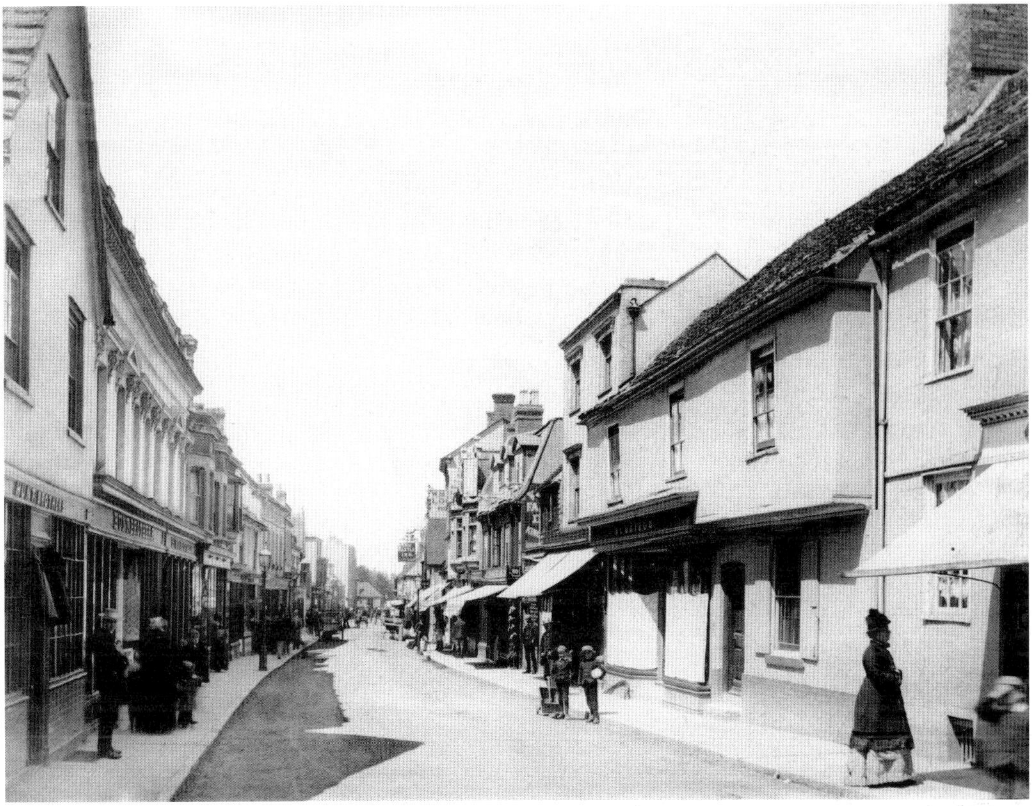

SALVAGE CORPS STATION
HORSHAM
CORPS.

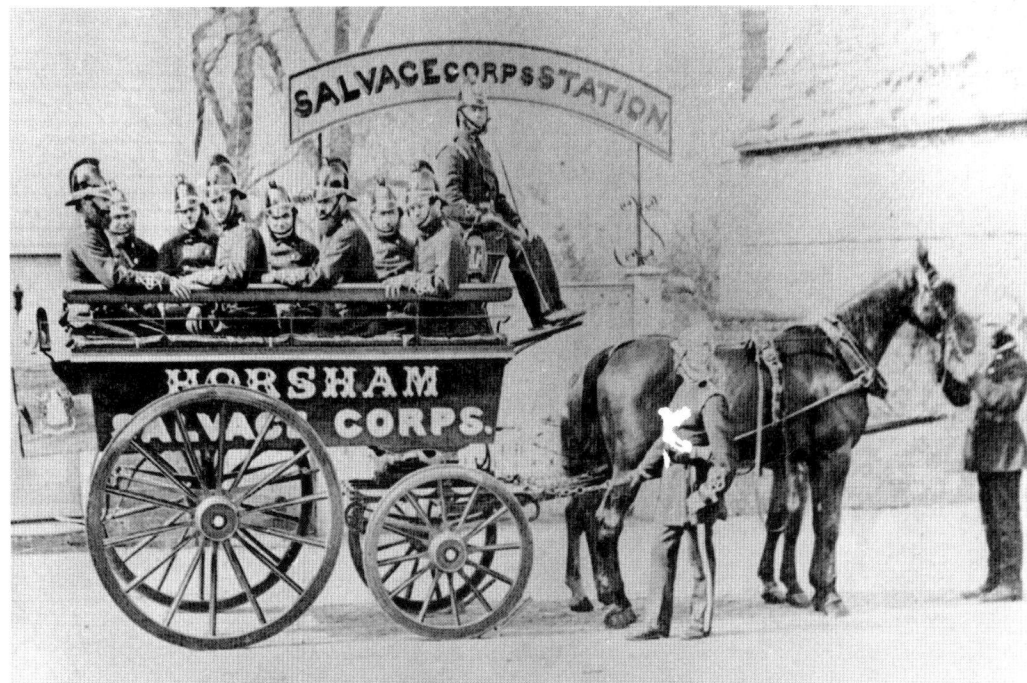

Lt Thomas Honywood in his uniform as Captain of the Volunteer Fire Brigade, a position he held for twenty-six years. He has already been mentioned as an early photographer, but he was also an artist, inventor and archaeologist. He discovered a hoard of medieval pottery when digging out the cellar of a new house he was building in West Street in 1867, and between 1870 and 1880 he excavated a number of barrows between Cocking and Bignor Hill.

Thomas was also the inventor of a process called 'Nature Printing', which he displayed at the International Inventions Exhibition in London in 1885. This was the business card that he had printed for this occasion.

Thomas Honywood's painting of his family home, Courtenay House, from Morth Gardens, shows that the passage through the house to the Causeway was then in a different position. Thomas married late in life, in 1878. This painting of his family probably dates from 1886, when his young son, Thomas Courtenay de Honywood, would be six years old, and his baby daughter Mabilia can perhaps be glimpsed in the arms of a nurse at the upper window. Thomas died in 1888, and his widow then married Leonard Henderson, Thomas's deputy in the Fire Brigade, who became the Deputy Chief Constable of West Sussex police.

Jury Cramp, here seen with his wife Mary, quickly made his mark in Horsham after his arrival in the 1870s, as a qualified goldsmith and watchmaker. He was a strong supporter of the Temperance movement, which tried unsuccessfully to play a part in local politics in the 1875 election. Jury established a Temperance Hotel in Market Square, but was not very popular with local landlords when he lectured them on the evils of drink!

This shows Jury Cramp's shop in West Street, next door to George Apedaile, the hatter, with William Hull's greengrocery and bakery on the far right of the photograph. The large spectacle sign hanging in front of Cramp's shop became a well-known feature of the town and is now in Horsham Museum. In the 1900s Jury Cramp diversified his activities and published some early photographs as a series of 'Old Horsham' postcards.

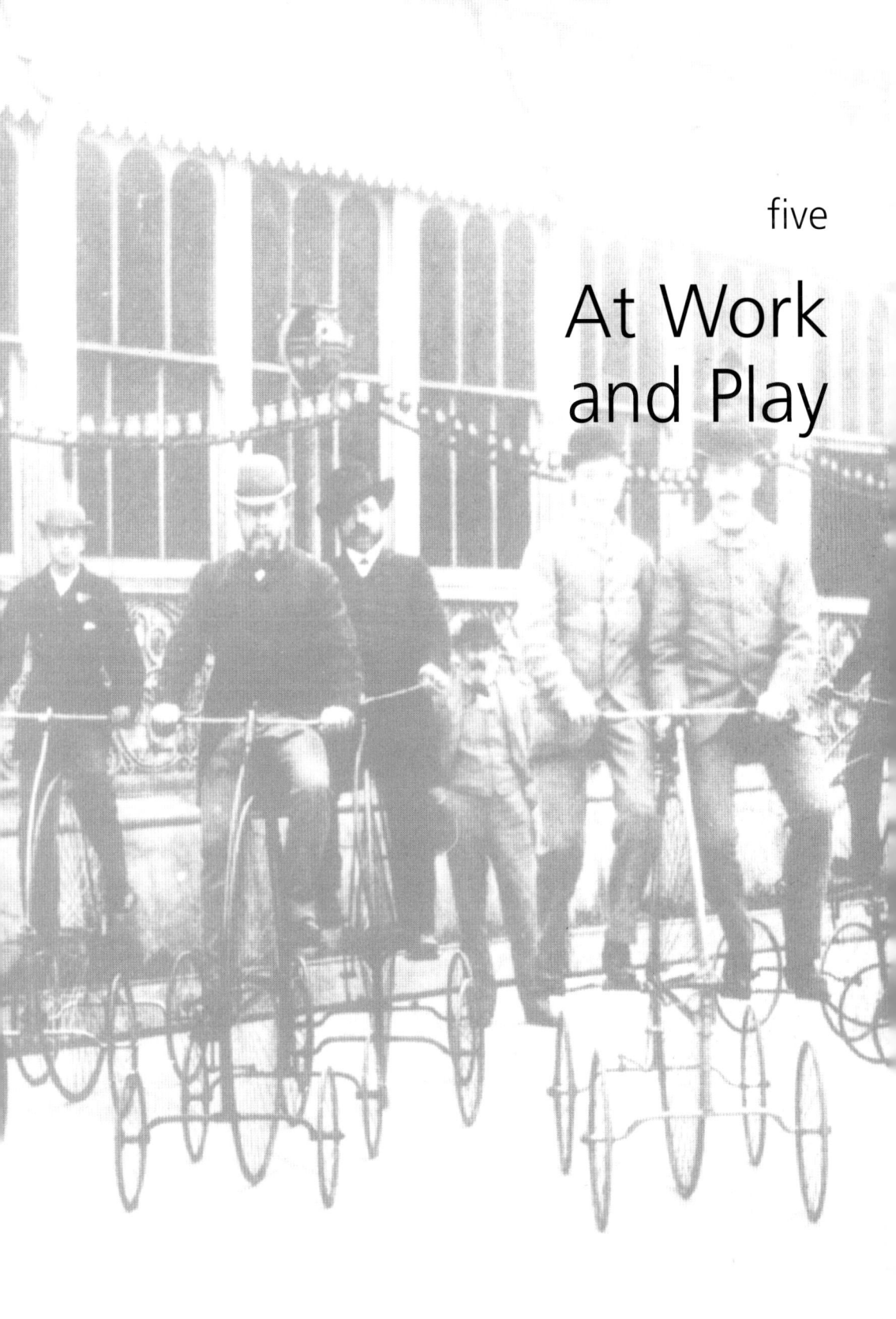

five

At Work
and Play

This postcard shows the Fire Brigade Procession and Gala on 7 July 1881, starting from the Queen's Head in Queen Street, which marked the forty-first anniversary of the founding of the Horsham brigade. The firemen can be seen on one of their engines and one man seems to have got up on to the inn sign to get a good view of the proceedings. A dinner followed, attended by guests from the Brighton and Worthing brigades, at which long speeches were made, and many toasts drunk.

Cricket was played in Horsham from the eighteenth century onwards, by gentry and tradesmen alike. In the 1830s, there was a cricket ground near the centre of the town, but in 1850, Horsham Cricket Club was given a piece of land off Worthing Road by Edward Tredcroft of the Manor House, where a Sussex team first played in 1853. The Horsham team for this match against Esher on 21 and 22 May 1888 included Clifton Brown, in the light-striped blazer, (probably the son of Major James Clifton Brown of Holmbush), and H.C. Attwater, on the far right, whose family kept a shop in Market Square.

This photograph, taken in 1886, is of the three young daughters of Henry Churchman, who had established a high-class grocery shop on the corner of Middle Street and South Street. The eldest girl Louisa, then aged eighteen, was to become a magistrate and local councillor in the 1920s, much admired for her judgement. She lectured at Workers' Educational Association classes, and the WEA Hall in North Street was later named after her. Her sister Emmeline helped her to work by acting as her housekeeper, while her other sister Maud became a qualified nurse.

The bicycle was one of the most useful inventions of the late nineteenth century, credited with doing more than anything else for the emancipation of women. But in its early days it appeared in a number of strange forms. The pentacycle was designed by the Horsham architect Edward Burstow in about 1883, and nicknamed the 'hen and chickens'. It was used by the General Post Office in London, and locally. Uncomfortable and difficult to steer, it was soon superseded by the 'safety' bicycle, which had gears and pneumatic tyres, in the 1890s. Nevertheless, this photograph shows some ten pentacycles in action, one of them a double-seater!

Mrs E. Seagrave's bakery in Springfield Road, photographed in the 1890s before it was rebuilt in a more imposing style on the corner of Springfield Road and the Bishopric. The two sisters, Mildred and Elizabeth Seagrave, are shown here with their niece, Ada Francis, and two bakers, Bob Maze and William Jackman. The bakery was set up by their parents in about 1850, so it could truly claim to be the 'old Horsham bakery' of its advertisements in the early 1900s.

The Seagrave bakery van is in the centre of this photograph of William Shaw's wheelwright's shop, which was conveniently situated next door to the blacksmith, J. Penfold, in London Road. They provided an essential service while everyone depended on horse-drawn transport.

Mrs Nightingale of Lambsbottom Farm in Hurst Road kept a dairy, and was a familiar figure as she drove around Horsham delivering her milk. The Nightingale family also had a brick works on the other side of Hurst Road, and another smallholding opposite the station.

An interesting photograph of Sam Davis, the last ropemaker in Horsham, listening to a gramophone. One wonders if this was the first time that he had seen such a machine, or whether it was his constant companion! Rope making in Horsham was mostly associated with saddlery. On the back of the photograph is a drawing of the little cart or caravan in which he travelled around. A small portrait bust of Sam Davis was made by George Mann, the son of Thomas the artist, and this is now in Horsham Museum.

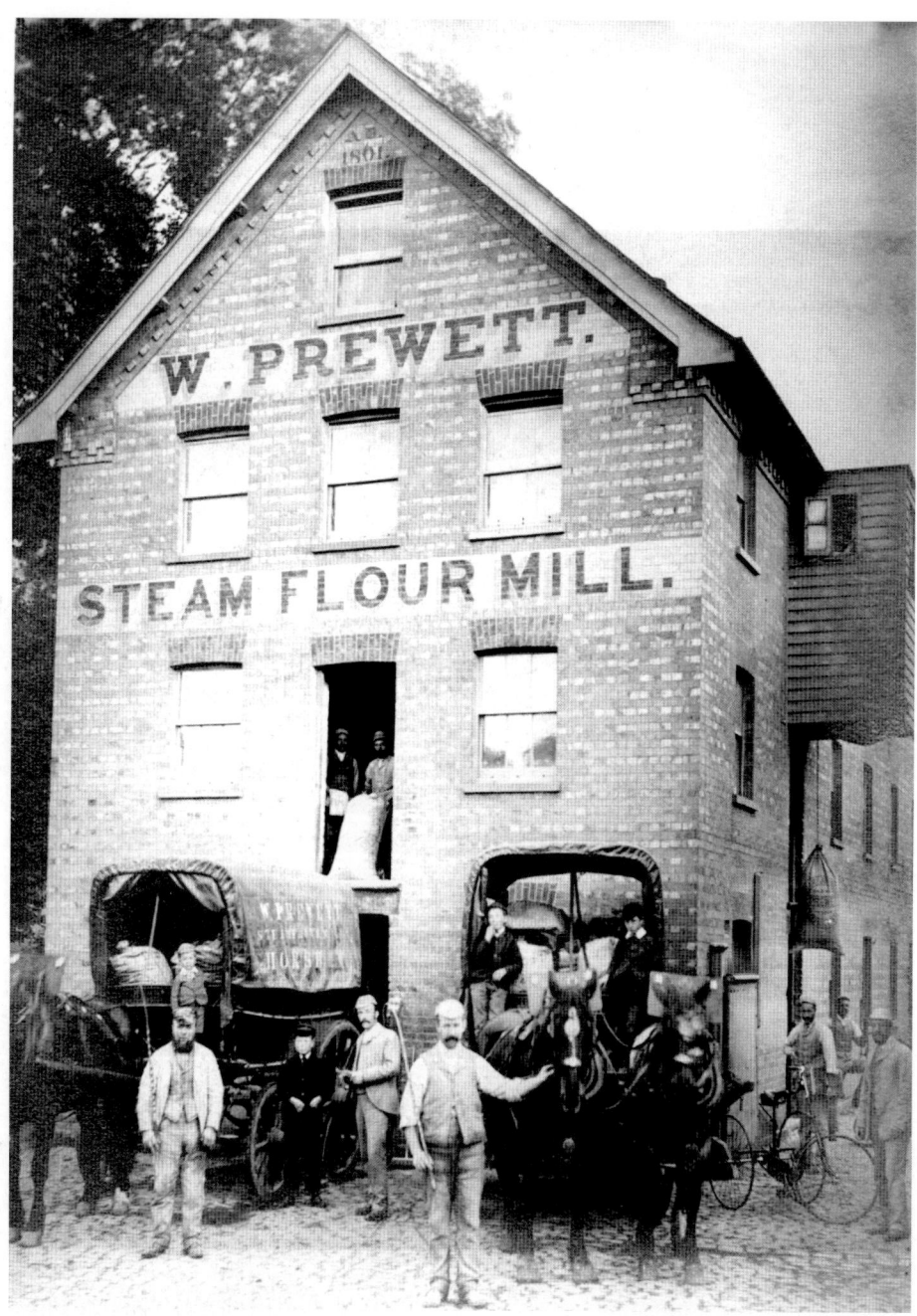

This photograph of Prewett's Mill near Tanbridge shows the entire staff going about their work. Sacks of meal are being hoisted to the upper floor on the right-hand side, and bags of flour are being loaded on to the two carts in the foreground. Prewett's Mill, built in 1861, used a steam engine as its main source of power, and later an electric motor. Most local mills were superseded in the late nineteenth century by large roller mills, but Prewett's Mill remained a flourishing operation, with its own bakery and shop in West Street, producing nearly 1,300 tons of stone-ground flour per week in the 1950s. It was taken over by Allinson's and closed in 1978.

The cattle market, held on alternate Wednesdays, was moved from the Carfax to the Bishopric in 1852. Animals were driven in from the surrounding farms. Cattle fairs came to an end during the First World War, but the market continued in the Bishopric until the 1920s when it was moved to the goods yard near Horsham station. This photograph shows a market day, probably in the 1890s, with traders and their customers mingling around the pens to do business.

An unusual view of the alleyway from Market Square to Middle Street, showing the back of Sendall's butcher's shop which had windows on both sides. There is a long row of hooks above the window of the house on the left – these were probably used to hang up poultry for display at Christmas time. Middle Street was known in the early nineteenth century as Butcher's Row, as it was then full of butchers' shops and slaughterhouses, conveniently situated near the cattle market in the Carfax.

An older Henry Padwick, junior, the magistrate and photographer, driving himself out of the Manor House in a smart carriage, in the 1890s. It must be a hot day as the horse has been thoughtfully provided with a sun-hat! Henry moved into the Manor House after his father's death in 1879, but was the last of his family to live there.

The parish almshouses in Normandy, founded by the Revd Jarvis Kenrick in 1844, are shown here about fifty years later with some of the residents enjoying their garden on a sunny summer's day. The original cottages had been extended or rebuilt, to accommodate four aged couples, as well as the fifteen widows or spinsters for whom the almshouses were originally intended. On saints' days, the residents received gifts from well-wishers. The smartly dressed young woman standing in the gateway may be a visitor or a helper.

Above: Skating was a popular diversion on Warnham millpond when the winter was cold enough – there were some very hard winters in the 1890s. But several tragedies occurred later when the ice gave way. By 1912, the Olympia Skating Rink in Queen Street, which was opened in 1876 for roller skating, had been converted into an ice-rink.

Right: The Salvation Army established a branch in Horsham on 10 February 1887 which has played an important part in the life of the town ever since. This photograph of a young couple in their Salvation Army uniforms, whose child seems ready to join the band, was probably taken in the early 1900s. However, the Army was not always welcomed when it first came to Sussex and there were riots in Worthing and Eastbourne where its espousal of temperance and the equality of the sexes within its ranks was seen as a 'foreign' threat to the traditional Sussex way of life.

David Price was a stationer in West Street who was involved in many aspects of Horsham life in the 1890s. A leading member of the Mutual Improvement Society, which had a hall in Albion Road where lectures and concerts were given, he was also the Honorary Librarian of the Free Christian Church. After the Horsham Museum Society was set up in 1893 to create a local town museum, David Price became the first Honorary Curator of its collections.

This photograph of the young William Albery shows the important part music played in his life. Despite having to run the family's long-established saddlery business in West Street and support his mother and seven sisters after his father's death in 1885, he found time to learn how to play the cornet. In 1900, he founded the Horsham Recreation Band, which later became the Horsham Borough Silver Band and competed successfully in many championships. Albery himself won the Southern Counties Championship as a solo cornet player, and made some early recordings on wax cylinders for Edison Bell phonographs.

This cartoon of Colonel (later Brigadier-General) Robert George Broadwood, the youngest son of Thomas Broadwood of Holmbush, depicts one of Horsham's military heroes. In 1901, on his return from the Boer War in South Africa, Horsham Urban District Council presented him with an illuminated scroll. In 1917, General Broadwood died from wounds received while serving on the Western Front. He was one of the highest-ranking officers to lose his life in active combat during the First World War.

The Revd Dr G.A. Thompson was the headmaster of Collyer's School when it was reopened as a boys' grammar school on a spacious new site in Hurst Road, in 1893. He was a distinguished scholar and a teacher whose pupils were well prepared to meet the challenges of the twentieth century. He retired in 1917, but the school continued to enjoy a strong reputation. Under the educational changes of 1974, it was once again reorganised, this time as a Sixth Form College.

This large group photo shows the residents of the Horsham Union Central Workhouse at the time of Queen Victoria's Diamond Jubilee in 1897. The men are all dressed identically in smocks and bowler hats and the women in tartan shawls. The workhouse was built in 1838 in Crawley Road, and in its early days it provided food, clothes and shelter for those who might otherwise have starved to death. In 1841, the majority of its inmates were children who had lost at least one parent, but by 1897 most were

old people. The workhouse was by then called the 'house of rest', doubtless to overcome the stigma still attached to such institutions. The Horsham Union was one of the first in the country to build a hospital attached to the workhouse, in 1867, for the treatment of the sick and poor. It was well supported by the local community, who organised concerts and other benefits for its residents.

At the dedication of the drinking fountain in the Carfax, to commemorate the 1897 Diamond Jubilee, many of Horsham's most notable townsfolk were gathered together. These have been identified, with one or two uncertain names, as follows. From left to right: Jury Cramp, A.M. Coleman, William Hull (junior), H.P. Thorpe (?), John Hicks (photographer), the Revd Bell (?), E.J. Perry, Arthur Aldridge, Robert Henry

Hurst, junior (who performed the ceremony), the Revd A.F. Young (curate, later Canon of Chichester), Alfred Agate (corn dealer), Canon Evan Daniel (Vicar), C.J. Stott, E.I. Bostock (magistrate), John Marsh (?), Samuel Mitchell (clerk to the newly formed Horsham Urban District Council), Thomas Richardson, Dr F. Kinneir, and William Lintott (wholesale grocer). Partly visible behind Canon Daniel is the Revd G.O. Frost (minister of the Congregational Church).

A general view of the Diamond Jubilee celebrations in the Carfax appears to show some of the gentlemen in the previous photograph standing on the bandstand, but it seems unlikely that the two photographs were taken on the same day. In this photograph, the drinking fountain is not yet in place,

but the Carfax is gaily decorated. The people all look well dressed and prosperous. Horsham, like the rest of the country, had benefited from the great expansion of trade and industry that marked Queen Victoria's later years.

This informal close-up of people meeting and chatting to their friends in the crowd also dates from the 1897 Jubilee celebrations. The bandstand, erected in 1892, can be seen in the background, and the decorations are the same as in the previous photograph.

This carnival float outside the Bedford Hotel shows the great pride Horsham people took in Britain and its empire at this period, heightened by the Boer War in South Africa, which lasted from 1899 to 1902. By now, many descendants of Horsham families were living in South Africa, Canada and Australia. Well-organised processions, band concerts, bazaars and charity balls were by now all part of the communal life of the town.

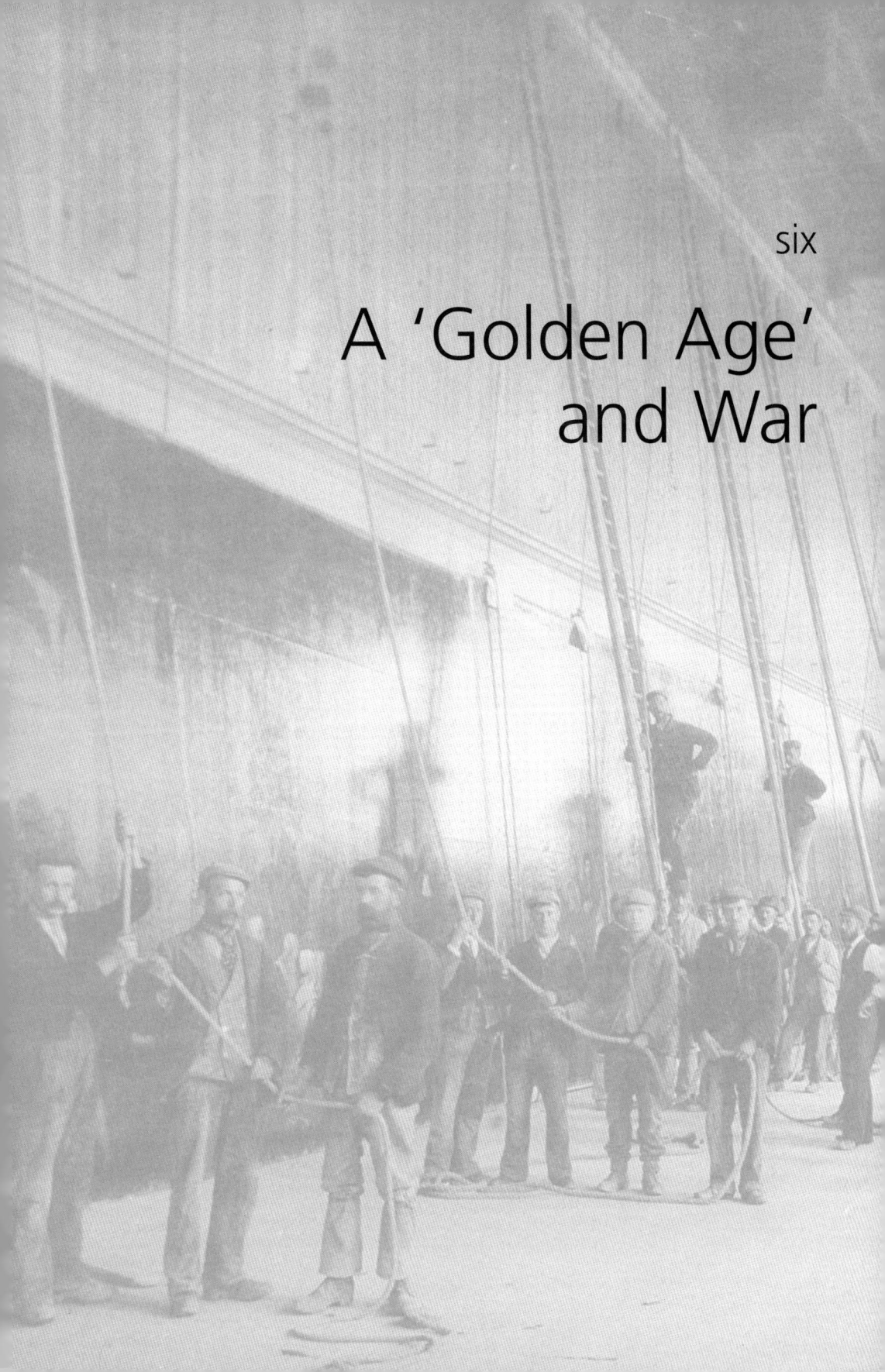

six

A 'Golden Age' and War

Above and below: The building of the new Christ's Hospital School on the Stammerham estate, just outside Horsham, required a large local workforce and acted as a boost to the emerging brick industry. In 1902, the great wall-painting by Antonio Verrio, of King Charles II granting a royal charter to the school in 1673, was moved from the old Great Hall of Christ's Hospital in London to its new home. The first photograph shows the eighty-five foot painting being lowered from its niche, by ropes and ladders. Then it was laid on the floor in sections, rolled up and transported to Horsham by the large horse-drawn wagon shown in the second picture, and successfully reinstalled in the new Dining Hall.

Laying Tables for Dinner, Christ's Hospital, Horsham

The Verrio wall painting can be seen in its new setting in this postcard. The Dining Hall is almost identical to the old Great Hall, with windows and doors that are similar in style and arrangement. Christ's Hospital boys quickly became a familiar sight in Horsham, and their band has taken part in many town celebrations during the last century.

King Edward VII had laid the foundation stone of Christ's Hospital in 1897, while still Prince of Wales, and he returned to Horsham to open the new school in 1902. Horsham townspeople are here seen pressing closely around his open carriage as it makes its way through the streets, but, in the excitement of the moment, not everyone is looking in the right direction!

HUNT BROTHERS.
COFFEE ROOM
WEST ST HORSHAM

AD HOTEL.
STABLES.
KING'S HEAD
HOTEL
MOTOR GARAGE
AND
INSPECTION PIT.
MOTOR
GARAGE

As this panoramic postcard shows, West Street, the main shopping street of Horsham, had been largely rebuilt by the early 1900s, and its shops now had large well-stocked windows to attract customers. This view can be compared with that on p.55.

Another panoramic view, of East Street from Market Square, shows that the King's Head Hotel had added a motor garage to its stables, to accommodate the growing number of its patrons who now came by car.

JUBILEE FOUNTAIN & CARFAX HORSHAM.

HORSHAM, NORTH STREET.

The striking new Bank Buildings in the Carfax were built in 1897 by Frederick Wheeler, a noted London architect, who established an office in Horsham. They replaced some of the old cottages with gardens that had previously formed a large part of the Carfax island. The Jubilee Fountain is a prominent feature in this photograph.

North Street became a residential street for wealthy professional men in the nineteenth century. The house on the right was successively occupied by the lawyer, Dewdney Stedman, his son William, who was Clerk to the Magistrates' Court, and later by Dr John Cayley Padwick. This part of North Street no longer exists, as it has been bisected by Albion Way, but Chart Way, the elevated pedestrian walkway past St Mark's Court, follows the line of the old street.

The entire indoor and outdoor staff of Coolhurst, a country house just outside Horsham, appear to be drawn up in this group photograph. Domestic service was the main form of work for most unskilled young women, but the staff of a large country house like this did perhaps have more

status and opportunities than other servants. The Coolhurst estate was owned in the early 1900s by C.R. Scrase Dickins, JP. The photograph shows something of the grandeur in which he, and other country gentlemen, lived at this period.

The Crawley and Horsham Hunt met at Sun Oak near Coolhurst in 1903. In the centre is the Revd E.D.L. Harvey, a local magistrate who lived at Beedingwood in Forest Road, and his daughter. Hunting was one of the main social activities of the many wealthy people who then owned large houses in and around Horsham.

This gleaming London Brighton & South Coast Railway engine, with its attendant railwaymen, is seen standing on a turntable outside the Horsham engine shed, which was constructed in 1896 as a semi-circular roundhouse. By now the railway company was a significant employer of men in Horsham, though agriculture and trade still predominated. The excellent train service made it possible for people living in Horsham to go to London for work, and Londoners to come and live in Horsham.

A line up of cars outside the King's Head Hotel in the Carfax in 1907 marks the coming of the new age of the motor car in Horsham, although their livery stables are still prominently advertised. Several local blacksmiths converted their premises to garages during the next few years.

This 1908 car accident at the foot of Rowhook Hill, off the road to Guildford, has drawn several spectators from among passing cyclists, but does not seem to have caused serious damage. A chauffeur, wearing a long dust coat, is seen on the right of the picture, with a gentleman who is probably the owner, waiting for the overturned car to be put to rights, by the men working in the background. The postcard was part of a series called 'Rural England', produced by Clifford Money, who lived in Slinfold from 1904 to 1926.

This photograph is said to be of the Horsham Caledonian Society at Beedingwood on 30 June 1910, but there is no evidence that such a society existed in Horsham at this time. It seems more likely that the group were members of the Caledonian Society of London,

who had come to Horsham for a summer outing with their families. They are all very well dressed, but none of the faces are familiar.

The musicians in this photograph were known as Mr Cook's Orchestra. The orchestra was formed and led by Raymond Cook, a music teacher, and it is known to have played on the Carfax bandstand and at the workhouse hospital in about 1910. Raymond Cook is in the centre of the photograph, and his wife is on the right of the front row. His father, who played the bass viol, is at the far right, and Fred and George

Chart, who were brothers of Mrs Cook, are in the back row. The girl to the left of Raymond Cook is Florrie Ireland, and her uncle, Bob Ireland, is behind her. Albert Garner, hairdresser of 21 East Street, Bob Gordon, of Spooner and Gordon, builders' merchants in London Road, Hubert Baker, who had a jeweller's shop in Queen Street, and Ernest Willett have been identified as other members of the orchestra.

Horsham played an active part in the Sussex Volunteer Corps, formed as a reserve after the Crimean War. The Horsham company was well trained in its own drill hall in Park Street, built in 1873 by Captain W. Egerton Hubbard of Leonardslee. By 1901, Horsham 'E' Company had a cyclists' section, seen in this photograph. In the back row are H. Hull, F. Hatchwell, H.H. Adams, 'Cought' Mills, and H.C. Attwater; in the middle row, F. Seagrave, G. Garner, Vern Dewdney, and Dan Lade, with R.M. King in front.

Horsham men would have attended the annual summer camp of the Royal Sussex Regiment Volunteers in Arundel Park in the early 1900s. Military training was being undertaken seriously by this time, and the Horsham 'E' Company became part of the 4th (Home Service) Reserve Battalion in 1908. In 1910 its HQ was moved from Worthing to Horsham. Henry, 15th Duke of Norfolk, is seen inspecting the camp, as commanding officer, with two of his children in 1911. (The little boy, Bernard, was to become the sixteenth duke and the Earl Marshal of England, who organised the coronation of Queen Elizabeth II in 1953.) When the First World War broke out in August 1914, the 4th Battalion was quickly reorganised for active service abroad.

This postcard, produced by the Bon Marché studio of Queen Street, shows soldiers marching through Horsham, watched by local residents, on their way to Europe. It is dated 10 September 1914, only five weeks after the start of the war. Were these troops from the local 4th Battalion or were they other soldiers simply passing through the town? In the next four years, Horsham men were to fight and die in Gallipoli, Egypt, Palestine and on the Western Front.

Food rationing was introduced in 1918, and by then women were having to take over work in factories and offices, as conscription had been brought in for all men of military age, in 1916, after heavy losses on the Western Front. This was the staff of the Horsham Food Office, who were in control of food supplies for the area. From left to right, back row: Cissie Holland, Winnie Charman, Flora White. Front row: Mabel McQuarrie Benn, Alice Redman, Gertrude Charman.

Beaulieu·Cottage·   Horsham·

Above and below: From the messages on the back of these postcards, it seems that a couple called Nell and Fred were living at Beaulieu Cottage, formerly the old Dog and Bacon Inn, in 1915. (Local directories confirm that a Fred Kent was living there between 1910 and 1915, next door to the new Dog and Bacon). Whether or not the intention was to show how people were coping on the home front, Nell and Fred seem to be quite self-sufficient, with apple trees, vegetables, chickens and maybe even rabbits in their garden. These are two more of Clifford Money's distinctive local postcards, with their black strip and white lettering.

&·Beaulieu·Cottage   Horsham·

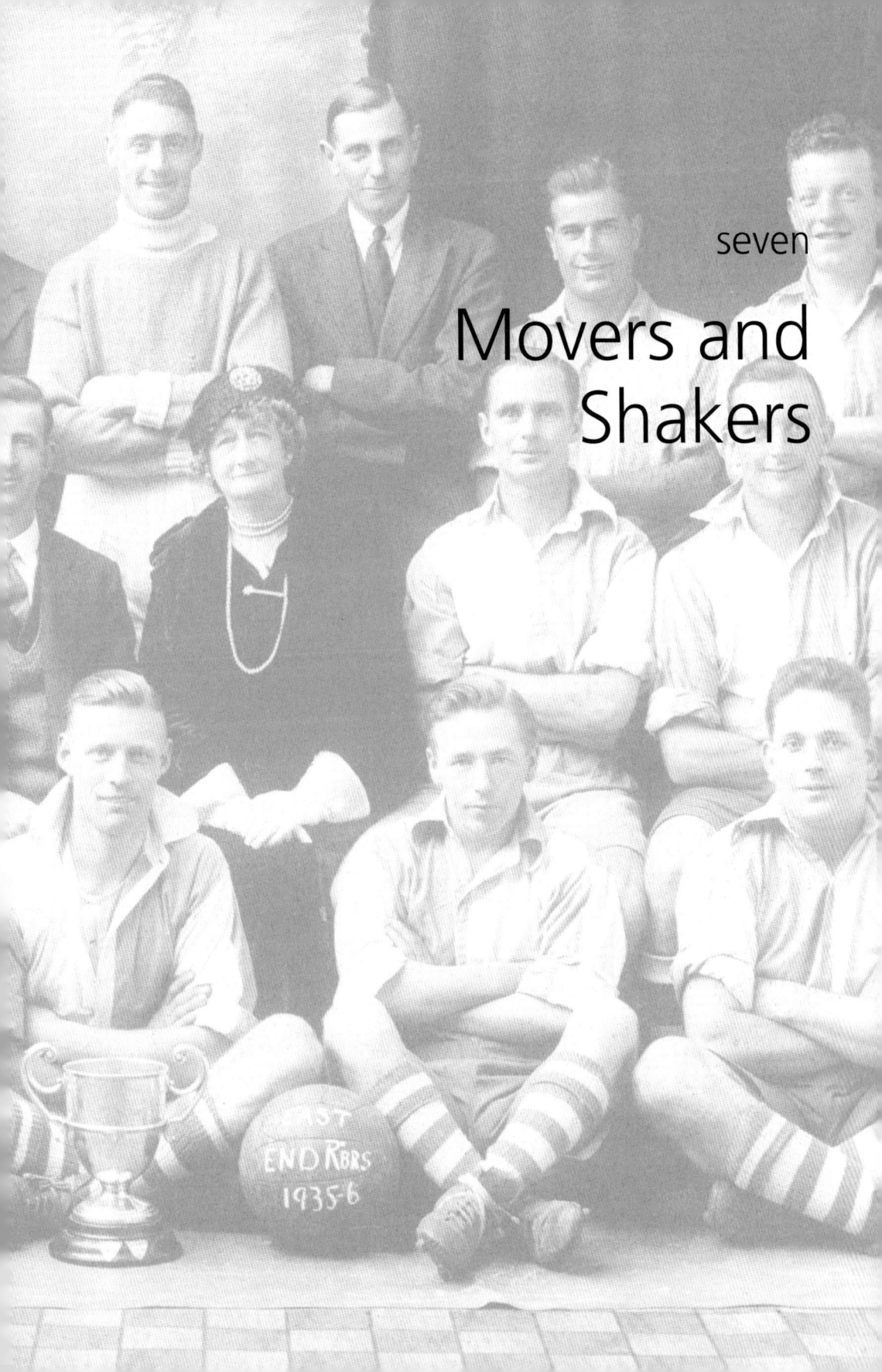

seven

Movers and
Shakers

With the return of peace, a rather bizarre contest took place in Horsham on 10 August 1919. Alfred Shrubb, the champion runner born in Slinfold, who broke seven world records in one night in 1904, was persuaded to run a five-mile race against a trotting horse called Kitty, which was watched by 2,300 spectators. His time was 28 minutes 8 seconds, but the horse, driven by Joseph Burton, was two minutes

faster! In this photograph taken outside the Bedford Hotel in Horsham, where the race started and finished, several members of the Hull and Parsons families have been identified among the crowd. Stan Parsons, later known as 'Mr Horsham', is the boy in the cloth cap near the dog in the front row.

Above: The effect of the war can be seen in this photograph of H. Rowland's stonemason's yard in Park Street, which probably dates from about 1920. The men are occupied in making war memorials for nearby villages, like Ashurst, for which there were considerable local fund-raising efforts at this time. There is something poignant about the old man and the little boy to the right of the picture. They remind us of a missing generation who had lost their lives in the First World War.

Below: In this photograph, probably taken in about 1920, a mixed group of young men and women are seen walking together down the Causeway. They are probably on their way to see the Sussex county team play during Horsham Cricket Week. This reflects a new spirit of companionship, which would probably not have been displayed so publicly in earlier times.

Above and below: The two photographs on this page actually come from an early film made in 1913, but the Cricket Week and Carnival procession became an even more important part of Horsham life during the inter-war years. The float shown below echoes the theme of that on page 76, but is more representative of the diversity of the people of the British Empire.

Above: Earl Winterton, first elected as MP for Horsham in 1904, represented the constituency for forty-six years, until 1950, as a Conservative committed to maintaining Imperial preference. During the First World War he served in the Middle East with T.E. Lawrence, and held office as Parliamentary Undersecretary for India in the 1920s. He was a member of Neville Chamberlain's cabinet for a short while in 1938 and became 'Father of the House' in 1945. He lived at Shillinglee Park, near Plaistow, and his main relaxation was fox-hunting.

Left: William Albery is seen here in his saddler's shop in West Street, in the 1920s, when he was also working on his monumental work, *A Parliamentary History of Horsham 1295-1885*, which was published in 1927. His saddlery collection and archive of documents relating to the town's history, which he collected over many years, are now in Horsham Museum.

Right: Major R.C.G. Middleton, MC, who lived in The Old House in London Road, set up the Blue Flash Association for demobilised men from the Royal Sussex Regiment soon after the First World War. He also became managing director of the Blue Flash Cinema Company, which employed ex-bandsmen to play in the orchestras that accompanied silent films at this period. This company built the Capitol Theatre in Horsham, which opened on 7 November 1923. Two other large cinemas, the Odeon and the Ritz, both part of nationwide chains, were built in North Street in the 1930s.

Below: The Capitol Theatre was designed by the Horsham architect Leslie H. Parsons, in Italian style, and quickly became a much-loved place of entertainment. It was used as a cinema as well as a theatre. It stood beside the old medieval burgage house of Bornes on what is now the site of the Swan Walk shopping mall. Both buildings, and the large gas holder behind them, have now been demolished as part of the redevelopment of the town centre in the last thirty years.

"The Capitol" Theatre, Horsham.

Left: The acquisition of Tanbridge House as a home for Horsham Girls' High School, in 1921, marked the beginning of a new educational era for Horsham girls. Miss Marchant, here seen with Miss Byles in the doorway, served as headmistress from 1921 to 1949, and under her guidance the school acquired an excellent reputation. As a result of the educational changes agreed in 1974, the school was converted into Tanbridge Comprehensive School. This has now moved to a modern building on Farthings Hill.

Below: A troop of Horsham Girl Guides, photographed in 1923. The Guides were a sister organisation to the Boy Scouts, founded by Lord Baden Powell, to train and inspire young people to serve the community. The Guide mistress is Miss I.M. Wigram, who later became Mrs Vernon. There are several members of the Cox, Stanford and Charman families among the girls.

Members of the Horsham Museum Society, who were at this time campaigning vigorously for a permanent home for their collections, on a visit to Lewes on 16 August 1928. At the invitation of Alderman J.H. Every (seated in the middle of the front row), the afternoon was spent at the Phoenix Iron Works, where Mr Every read a paper and conducted the visitors around his museum. The Horsham Museum Society group was led by Samuel Mitchell (standing behind Mr Every), and included William Albery, who can be seen third from the left in the back row.

Sir Cecil Hurst, son of Robert Henry Hurst, a distinguished lawyer who was a member of the International Court of Justice from 1929 to 1945, is seen here as President of Horsham Museum Society at Park House in 1930. In 1929, two rooms were allocated for the display of the collections built up by Horsham Museum Society since 1893, after William Albery had stood for the council in pursuit of this aim. Dr M.H.H. Vernon, on the left of Sir Cecil, was the speaker at the opening of Horsham Museum in its first official home.

Brick making became a major industry in Horsham in the early twentieth century, with large brickworks owned by the Sussex Brick Company in Warnham and Southwater. This Ruston steam excavator, bought for the Warnham brickworks at a cost of £1,250, was moved to Southwater in 1929, where it was still in service in 1947. Note the girl in the bucket! The fossilised bones of an iguanadon were dug out of the lower depths of the Southwater clay pit during the Second World War.

James Stewart Whitehouse, who is second left in the front row, was appointed manager of the Warnham branch of the Sussex Brick Company in 1903. His brother, Duncan Haydn Whitehouse, on the far left, became works manager in 1912. After a period of rapid expansion, the Sussex Brick Company became a public company in 1927. This photograph of the directors was probably taken at about this time.

Many improvements in brick-making technology were introduced in the 1920s. This photograph marked the installation of a Davey Paxman steam generator on 10 June 1925. On the same day, J.S. Whitehouse successfully fired the first kiln-fired machine-made stock bricks in a new Staffordshire kiln at Southwater.

The Southwater Brick Works had distinctive 175ft high chimneys which dominated the village, but the name 'Southwater Bricks' was painted out in 1939, to avoid identification from the air by German pilots. There was one air attack on the works in 1942, when a train driver was killed, but otherwise little damage was done. The Southwater Works were closed down in 1982, and a country park has now been created around the old clay pit.

This Cricket Week procession through the Carfax in 1933 was watched by a happy and relaxed looking group of townspeople, despite the fact that this was a period of great economic depression. The Horsham Unemployment Committee decided in 1933 to redirect its fundraising efforts to provide work instead of monetary relief. Horsham Urban District Council agreed to build a swimming pool, for which there was a growing demand, using unemployed labour.

In this view of the empty central marketplace, to the east side of the Carfax, also taken in 1933, the Victorian cottages built by William Pirie can be seen in the background. Horse-drawn carts are still in use, as well as motor vehicles, as the tidying up is done.

Many of Horsham's outlying villages and farms were still without piped water in the 1930s.
A water cart is seen here at Broadbridge Heath, in the summer of 1934. The water was sold
at a halfpenny per bucket, and it was delivered twice a day by the Horsham Urban District
Council. George Etheridge, who is shown as distributing the water, later became foreman at the
Broadbridge Heath sewage works. Among the ladies are Mrs Walker and Mrs Potter, the wife of
the policeman at Broadbridge Heath. Among the men are Mr Highgate (formerly a milkman) and
Mr G. Lawrence, in the doorway of the post office, where he was employed.

This photograph shows 'Omick' Whitehead, a 'hommiker' who mixed 'pug' clay and fine ashes to
make clamp bricks in Nightingale's brickyard, outside his cottage in Grub Street, in about 1935.
He worked as a costermonger as a sideline at weekends and at holiday time. Grub Street, now part
of an extended Highlands Road, seems to have acquired its earlier name because it was often very
muddy. Children were warned to keep away from it on wet days!

The opening of Horsham's first municipal swimming pool on 7 July 1934 was an impressive occasion. Sir Ofori Atta, an hereditary Paramount Chief and member of the Legislative Council of the Gold Coast, had been invited to perform the ceremony and was resplendent in his tribal robes, shaded by a large umbrella. David Bryce, the chairman of Horsham Urban District Council, who is standing beside him,

was the first to dive into the pool, 'amid loud applause'. There was a fine display of diving and swimming by local teams. In the first week, 3,750 bathers passed through the turnstiles and the pool quickly became established as a most important part of Horsham's social scene, especially for young people.

Mrs Nellie Laughton, in the centre of this photograph, was Horsham's first woman councillor and an important figure in Horsham in the years between the wars. She created a Garden of Remembrance by the river, which she gave to the town, and played a catalytic role in the campaign for a new swimming pool. Here she is seen with the East End Ramblers' football team, which won the Horsham Senior Charity Cup in the 1935/36 season.

W.H.Bernard Lintott, chairman of Horsham Urban District Council in 1937, was a prominent figure who was active in his support of Horsham Art School, the museum, the swimming pool and many other local causes. His father, William Lintott, had successfully developed a wholesale grocery business on the west side of the Carfax, and also founded the Lintott engineering works, which became an important local company, producing munitions during the Second World War, and precision engineering after 1945.

Above: Dr John Cayley Padwick, one of the sons of Henry and Jane Padwick, is seen here planting a tree in Horsham Park in 1935. Louisa and Emmeline Churchman are in the background, behind the tree. Dr Padwick served in the Royal Army Medical Corps and was a general practitioner in Bridgnorth, Shropshire, during his medical career. He became a well-known figure in Horsham during his later years. The Parkside building, headquarters of the Royal & Sun Alliance Group, now occupies the site of his house and garden in North Street.

Below: The staff of Horsham Institution (formerly the Horsham Workhouse) and Hospital in the 1930s. Mr H.W. Fry, sitting in the centre of the front row, with his wife on his right, were the last Master and Matron. Nurse Noonan, on his left, was in charge of the nursing staff, and Frederick Wheatland, standing behind her, was the labour master of the casual wards. The Institution was closed in 1939, but both buildings were used by the Canadians as a base hospital during the Second World War.

Manor House School, established in the Manor House on the Causeway, was one of the leading private preparatory schools in Sussex between the wars. The novelist, Hammond Innes, was a pupil there in the 1920s. This school photograph, taken in 1937, shows a high proportion of staff to pupils.

Above: The new CIBA laboratories, here seen in an architectural drawing, were built in Horsham in 1939. The arrival of this Swiss pharmaceutical company in Horsham was of great importance to the local economy, which the council was actively seeking to diversify into light engineering and other industries.

Opposite above: The local branch of the Royal Observer Corps, seen here outside the drill hall in Denne Road, played a crucial role in tracking enemy aircraft and V1 rockets passing over Sussex on their way to bomb London during the Second World War. A few stray bombs fell on Horsham and some German planes crashed nearby, but in general the town was lucky enough to escape serious damage or great loss of life.

Below: The Hewell family, shown here in a photograph by E.W. Copnall, were fully engaged in the war effort. The two elder sons served in the Royal Corps of Signals and the Royal Navy. Mr Hewell was an air-raid warden often on duty through much of the night, while also working as a coachbuilder at Rice Brothers during the day. Mrs Hewell was a cook in the canteen run by the women's voluntary service for the Canadian soldiers who were camped on Denne Hill, and both she and her husband were members of the British Legion.

Left: Ernest Dieter Ball, a young Jewish refugee from Germany, was evacuated from London to Horsham in 1941, and stayed for a year before being sent to Canada. His letters to his parents, which have now been published, are a valuable sidelight on life in the town during this period, and he retained warm memories of his stay in Horsham for the rest of his life.

Above right and right: Victory in Europe Day celebrations in May 1945 were spoilt by the weather. Although tables were spread in Albion Terrace for a street party, the rain forced everyone to take shelter in the gas works building. It looks as if there is a pony among the people crowding through the door! Though rather poor in quality, these photographs record a historic and happy day.

eight

Change and Renewal

A proud group of Warnham brick workers celebrate the production of one million bricks per week in 1948. The Horsham brick industry reached its peak in the years after the Second World War, with the huge demand for new housing. Large numbers of people moving out of London led to a forty per cent increase in the population of Horsham between 1939 and 1961.

An old-fashioned steam engine in fine condition is an object of interest for a group of schoolboys in this 1948 photograph. In the foreground, a former engine driver from Horsham, then aged eighty-eight, is posing beside one of the engines he had driven for many years previously. Nicknamed 'General' Jackson, he was too tall to get into the cab and used to stand on the footplate. Dr Beeching's cuts in the rail network in the 1960s meant that Horsham lost the line to Guildford, as well as a link to Shoreham and Brighton.

The austerities of the war years continued into the 1950s, along with the barbed wire, as shown in this rather stark photograph taken in Horsham Park in 1951 by a member of the Horsham Photographic Society. But the establishment of the National Health Service and other reforms greatly improved the real quality of life for many people in Horsham, as was the case elsewhere.

Empty building sites hidden by advertising hoardings in East Street are shown in this photograph. There was considerable redevelopment of this part of East Street, and large new housing estates, on the north and east sides of the town, were built to accommodate the large increase in population in the 1950s and 1960s.

These houses in Park Street look shabby and old fashioned, while the Carfax was becoming choked with increasing traffic. The rapid growth of Crawley as a new town, and the growing importance of Gatwick airport, led Horsham businessmen to campaign vigorously for significant improvement of the town's facilities in the 1960s. It was decided to build a new main road around the Carfax, and a modern shopping centre to be called Swan Walk.

William Stanley Parsons, BEM, who had a newsagent's business in the Carfax, was a very important figure in the town both during and after the Second World War. Here he is seen with the award given to him for raising enough money to build a Spitfire. He served as an independent councillor and was nicknamed 'Mr Horsham' in recognition of his tireless involvement in all aspects of the town's life. An alley off East Street has been named 'Stan's Way' after him.

David Bryce, leading tradesman, councillor, governor of Collyer's School, Secretary of the swimming club and its chief examiner for swimming and life-saving awards, was another man who was deeply involved in practically everything that went on in Horsham. This photograph was taken in 1952. He founded the David Bryce Club in New Street, which now caters for elderly people.

Dr Geoffrey Sparrow came to Horsham in 1919 and joined a local medical practice, but also found time to indulge his love of hunting and drawing in pen and ink. In his retirement he was able to devote more time to art. His many pictures of huntsmen and hunting are in a long British tradition of sporting caricature, but he also drew local scenes and animals. Here he is seen with his wife, who ran a farm at Maplehurst, where they lived in the 1950s.

Harold Saunders Smith, pharmacist, was a familiar figure in the old-fashioned chemist's shop of Williams and Smith in West Street. Some of its contents – the drug drawers, some gold-labelled pharmacist's bottles and many other small items – are now on display in Horsham Museum. They were acquired when the shop was eventually sold in 1972.

Above: G.F.W. Hart, MA (Oxon), retired history teacher at Collyer's School, served as Honorary Curator of Horsham Museum from 1949 to 1964. Here he is seen with B.F. Pay, the Honorary Secretary of Horsham Museum Society, examining some sixteenth century frescoes discovered at the premises of Hoad and Taylor in Market Square. This building, which was originally part of the old Talbot and Wonder burgage, was used by Jury Cramp as his Temperance Hotel. Later it became the Old Waverley Hotel, run by Emma Hull who had earlier managed the Crown Inn.

Left: Two Collyer's boys on a visit to Horsham Museum in the 1950s are seen with a 'scold's bridle'. In the background can be seen the old town stocks and the original ring used for bull-baiting. The museum was given a permanent home in Causeway House in the late 1940s, after active campaigning by Sir Cecil Hurst and William Albery. It was taken over by Horsham Urban District Council in 1966 and professional curators were appointed. It is now considered to be one of the best small local museums in the country.

Above: Horsham's fine tradition of municipal bands has continued. The Horsham Borough Silver Band is here seen giving the August festival concert at the Capitol Theatre in 1959.

Right: The Queen Mother with the Revd Peter Gillingham, Vicar of St Mary's church, coming to open the new St Mary's Primary School on 25 March 1965. The school was built near the church, on the site of the first Collyer's School, where Horsham children have now been taught for over four centuries.

This shows the inner courtyard of Swan Walk as it was built in the early 1970s, after the demolition of the old burgage house called Bornes. In the late 1980s it was extended over the site of the former Capitol Theatre, roofed over, and converted into a modern shopping mall.

The Sun Alliance and London Insurance Co. leased Stocklund House, a skyscraper built as a commercial development on the site of Dr Padwick's house in North Street, as their administrative headquarters in 1964. It was pulled down and rebuilt as Parkside House in 1992. As part of the redevelopment of the Carfax area, Sun Alliance, working with Horsham District Council, created a 'campus' of new buildings around an extended Albion Way in the late 1980s, and became the largest employer in the town in the 1990s.

Right and below: Councillor Marjorie Ward, chairman of Horsham District Council, cutting the tape at the opening of the second part of Albion Way, on 27 September 1990. This passed under the new St Mark's Court and linked North Street and East Street. Christ's Hospital Band (which by then included girls) was there to mark the occasion.

Left: Martin Pearson, the chief executive of Horsham District Council from 1974 to 2005, is the man chiefly responsible for masterminding the redevelopment of the town centre in the last thirty years. Horsham was listed as the top 'boom town' of Britain in 1990, and over £200 million had been invested in its economy by 2005.

Below: The Carfax remains the place where Horsham people gather on public occasions. On Remembrance Sunday in 1992, councillors and representatives of various local organisations took part in an open-air service, conducted by Canon Derek Tansill, the Vicar of St Mary's church. This is one of a series of photographs taken by Ray Luff on this occasion.

Gordon Road celebrated its Golden Jubilee in 2002 with a party for all its residents. There is a growing pride in their identity by small local communities within the town that now has a population of more than 30,000 people.

A sundial which celebrates the long history of Horsham and its district, created by the distinguished sculptors Lorne McKean and her husband, Edwin Russell, catches the dawn sunlight as it is lowered into place in the new Forum. This striking piece of public art was unveiled by the Queen, who visited Horsham on 24 October 2003 with the Duke of Edinburgh, to mark the third and final phase of the town centre redevelopment. She also opened the refurbished Arts Centre, now renamed the Capitol, as a tribute to the earlier theatre. Horsham has not forgotten its past as it enters the twenty-first century as a modern community.

Other local titles published by Tempus

Horsham Then & Now
HORSHAM MUSEUM SOCIETY AND HORSHAM PHOTOGRAPHIC SOCIETY

This book takes a nostalgic look at some of the well-loved buildings and streets of Horsham and depicts the local farms, industries and businesses as they used to be, alongside modern photographs showing the changes which have taken place.

0 7524 2445 9

Billingshurst and Wisborough Green
WENDY LINES

This fascinating collection of over 200 archive photographs and postcards charts the development of Billingshurst and Wisborough Green, two adjacent Wisborough parishes. The rural heritage of the parishes is well illustrated, as are the lives of ordinary people – in churches, schools, businesses and recreation, and in peace times and war.

0 7524 2482 3

Sussex CCC – Fifty of the Finest Matches
JOHN WALLACE

Sussex County Cricket Club, the oldest of the county clubs, have been playing cricket since time immemorial, although trophies have been relatively few and far between. For all that, classic matches certainly do abound. John Wallace recounts some of the most memorable matches which Sussex have played.

0 7524 2379 3

Young Jim – The Jim Parks Story
DEREK WATTS

Jim Parks was the most successful member of a Sussex cricketing dynasty that also included his father 'Old Jim', and his uncle Harry. First appearing for the county in 1949, he was a handsome stroke player, dashing cover fielder and useful leg-spin bowler, who later became one of the great early wicketkeeper-batsmen, playing forty-six times for his country. This book, the first authorised biography of 'Young Jim', is a fascinating read and a fitting tribute to one of the county's best loved cricketing sons.

0 7524 3550 7

If you are interested in purchasing other books published by Tempus, or in case you have difficulty finding any Tempus books in your local bookshop, you can also place orders directly through our website

www.tempus-publishing.com